Texts in Computing

Volume 12

The Mathematics of the Models of Reference

Texts in Computing Series Editor
Ian Mackie   mackie@lix.polytechnique.fr

The Mathematics of the Models of Reference

Francesco Berto
Gabriele Rossi
and
Jacopo Tagliabue

ISBN 978-1-84890-011-0

College Publications
Scientific Director: Dov Gabbay
Managing Director: Jane Spurr
Department of Computer Science
King's College London, Strand, London WC2R 2LS, UK

http://www.collegepublications.co.uk

Original cover design by Richard Fraser
Cover produced by orchid creative   www.orchidcreative.co.uk
Printed by Lightning Source, Milton Keynes, UK

Table of Contents

... in memory of Alan Mathison Turing
(London, June 1912 - Wilmslow, June 1954)

Foreword

The *mathematics of the models of reference* has been formulated at iLabs Milan, a private research lab in applied Artificial Intelligence devoted to the achievement of the indefinite extendibility of human life-span. It has been developed via a series of successive extensions, starting with an imaginative insight. We have envisaged it mainly as a tool – with no special prize to win, position to conquer, or possible fundraising in mind: we just needed it as an instrument. One needs a fridge in order to preserve one's food; a hammer in order to hammer nails; and a mathematics that can recapture previously developed mathematical techniques, in order to completely reproduce the human mind. An ambitious task indeed – but once the indefinite extendibility of life has been assumed as possible, as we do in our lab, no cognitive endeavor can be frightening *a priori*.

The possible applications of the mathematics of the models of reference are of major importance to us: as we begin to show in the book, it should not only recapture other kinds of mathematics, but also allow us to represent a possible model of the physical universe itself – a model that does not contradict our current, established experimental and scientific knowledge. It should also allow us to describe our mind's cognitive activities, including those relating to such fields as creativity, intuition, and emotions.

We expect readers interested in computation in general to be puzzled by such a framework. However, if we provisionally assume that, at the bottom level of reality, "everything behaves alike", our theoretical option might not look so bizarre. Mathematics is one of the most fascinating human enterprises, but from our viewpoint it is, first of all, the tool to understand the behavior of reality, as well as of our mind investigating reality – perhaps in order to win the prize of the endless extension of human life-span.

The *Introduction* of our book informally presents the theoretical pillars of our theory, to be developed in subsequent Chapters: the notion of *Model of Reference* (for which we will often use the abbreviation "MoR" for convenience, without distinction between singular and plural) which is – behind a somewhat unusual terminology – the general idea of a deterministic, algorithmic operator; and the *discrete universe* hypothesis, which we take from such classic – albeit non-standard – approaches to the physics of computation as Stephen Wolfram's *New Kind of Science*, Konrad Zuse's works, and the by now well-established theory of *cellular automata*.

In *Chapter 1*, we describe the cellular automaton developed in our lab. We explore some of its basic mathematical features, highlighting in particular the *strong reversibility* of its dynamic rule, i.e., the fact that not only distinct initial states in the evolution of the automaton lead to distinct final states, but also, any configuration of the automaton can be regained by running it backwards via the very *same* dynamic rule. Strong reversibility, as we explain there, is highly desirable both for theoretical and for practical reasons.

Next, we show how, by implementing such a rule, the automaton is capable of universal computation, i.e., it can simulate a universal Turing machine and compute (if Turing's Thesis is right) anything computable, insofar as each cell of the automaton acts as a *universal* and *reversible* logical gate. The strategy we follow is the same as the one used by Berkelamp, Conway and Guy in their constructive proof that Conway's celebrated cellular automaton, *The Game of Life*, is computation-universal: it consists in showing how all the basic building bricks of computation (memory, circuits, logical gates) can be emulated by patterns and configurations of (states of) the elementary cells of the automaton.

Chapter 2 introduces the formal symbolism used in the following: this is the canonical notation of first-order logic with identity and function symbols. The choice of the standard notation of elementary logic in a mathematical book is theoretically motivated: in the development of the book, the principles of our theory are introduced as non-logical, first-order axioms that work as constraints on the admissible models, whereas the rules of first-order logic (the chosen form is classical natural deduction), being sound and complete, in principle allow one to infer all the axioms' logical consequences.

Chapter 3 presents, in the form of a set of such axioms, the *formal ontology* underlying our automaton. This is a mereological framework describing a discrete, finite physical universe. Its main features are its being atomistic (no "atomless gunks"), hyper-extensional (identity of parthood entailing identity *tout-court*), and characterized by unrestricted mereological composition. Some basic notions of our universe, such as *sequentiality, system, internal, external,* are defined starting with the initial formal axioms.

Chapter 4 imports *classical recursion theory* into our model: given that our MoR are deterministic operators on discrete quantities, this is quite a natural move. After introducing some basic notions of function theory, such as the ones of *partial* and *inverse* operator, we show how positive integers can be represented as cell state configurations in our automaton, in a way analogue to their appearing as sequences of tallys in the tape of an ordinary Turing machine. Next, we show how such configurations of states, together with the dynamical rule animating our automaton, can provide physical realizers for (or, as philosophers say, "ramseyfy") the basic functions of recursion theory, such as the zero function or the projection functions. More complex operators can then be defined starting with the basic ones via the standard recursive procedures. By importing in our framework the classic and well-known results of basic recursion theory, such interesting concepts as the notion of a *meta*-MoR, that is, of an operator taking as inputs the codes of other operators and simulating them, can be precisely defined.

The short *Chapter 5* provides quick hints at possible algebraic developments of the theory, together with some considerations on the relevance of the notion of isomorphism, as applied to our theory of the MoR.

The *Appendices* point at some possible, and in our view interesting, extra-matematical developments of the theory. *Appendix I* includes some initial and tentative conjectures on the connections between our formal theory and computational linguistics. The framework, though, is classically logical and, indeed, model-theoretic. We believe that Montague-style grammar still is the best approach to computationally tractable semantics and, following such classic works as Chierchia-McConnell-Ginet's *Meaning and Grammar*, we highlight its virtues.

Appendix II is an excursus on a promising technological spin-off: we highlight the connections between our computational model and some recent discoveries in the field of nanotechnology. As we explain there, researches have begun to show how such nanomaterials as *graphene* (one-atom thick layers of graphite with peculiar physical features) can actually implement cellular automata. *We* begin to show that the resulting physical implementation is strikingly similar to our cellular model.

Appendix III is an overview of the new and rapidly growing field of *system biology*: following Dennis Bray's recent and wonderful book *Wetware*, we show how thinking of the physics and chemistry of living cells in terms of discrete implementation of deterministic operators, i.e., MoR, can provide interesting insights into the world of microbiology.

The Mathematics of the Models of Reference has a companion web site (in Italian and in English):

www.mmdr.it

This includes 2D and 3D simulations of the cellular automata considered in the book, plus interactive tutorials, free software, and extra material.

Finally, as non-native English speakers, we are very grateful to Camilla Peroni for smoothly translating and revising the original version of this book

Francesco Berto
Gabriele Rossi
Jacopo Tagliabue

www.iLabs.it

Introduction

Our approach builds upon these two basic ideas: (1) a strong isomorphism between physical and informational reality, and (2) an extensive development of the notion of *model of reference* – a truly fundamental concept we are to gradually explain, and whose treatment occupies most of the book you are holding in your hands.

As is well-known, research projects on Artificial Intelligence (AI) are founded on the convinction that the fuzzy aggregate of abilities we call "intelligence" can be realized artificially, in particular, as an algorithm. For those who believe in AI to think is to compute, that is to say, to elaborate information by operating on data through effective algorithmic procedures.

It is generally conceded that an algorithm capturing the vast spectrum of activities pertaining to the human mind would be very different from the current, ordinary computer programs. However complicated, though, it would still be an algorithm; thus, it could be implemented as software in an information processing device having sufficient speed and power.

There are many general philosophical objections to the idea of Artificial Intelligence itself (two among all: the so-called "göedelian arguments", put forward by such authors as J.R. Lucas and Roger Penrose; the Chinese Room argument devised by the philosopher John Searle). However, the actual, *practical* diffculties facing AI are of two rather precise kinds: (1) first, one has to find or construct the appropriate information processing device having sufficient speed and power; (2) next, one needs to have a more accurate idea of what the aforementioned fuzzy set of capacities realized in our mind, and that we label "intelligence" – but of which we presently have only qualitative, mostly analogical, if not metaphorical characterizations – consists of (think of Dennett's *intentional stance* view).

It is exactly on these two points that the aforementioned ideas underlying the research conducted in our laboratory are set in motion, that is to say, the physics-information isomorphism, and the theory of the models of reference (MoR).

The starting point of our investigation is the idea that an effective and exhaustive description of reality must be based on a structural identity between the physical world and the informational dimension at all levels. Such insight is at the core of the formal theory we will develop in the present volume: (a) on the one hand, we deem information and its elaboration to be rooted in physical reality from its most elementary level; (b) on the other hand, the physical universe is to be seen essentially as an information processor and organizer. One could describe everything that occurs in the world in the most concise manner by saying: what the whole universe does is computing, at every instant of time, its next overall state at the subsequent instant. If this surprises you or seems elusive, doubts might be dissipated as such notions as *universe*, *instant* (and even *computing*) are more precisely characterized in the following pages; for the time being, a first intuitive approach will suffice.

Following this basic insight, we are convinced that the construction of artificial super-intelligence will not be *that* artificial – in other words, we believe that the information processing device having sufficient speed and power is not unattainable: such device already exists, it is not artificial because it is in nature; and it is so because *universal computation is embedded in the ultimate essence of reality*, of the universe itself, from its last and elementary dimensional level – as we will conjecture in more detail in the first Chapter of the volume.

As far as the second point of our research is concerned, specifically, the clarification of the notion of "intelligence", this is where the notion of *model of reference* comes into play. We present here a first, intuitive characterization: a model of reference (MoR) is basically nothing but a temporally ordered sequence: <perception → thought → action>.

Is that it? In some sense, yes. Nevertheless, in some other sense, the definition of the MoR as sequences of perceptions, thoughts, actions, lacking further qualifications can be misguiding, leading us to believe that the MoR are just psychological structures. The MoR, instead, are *also*, but not exclusively, this; however we believe that the MoR are realized, or, as it is said in computer science and AI contexts, "implemented" in the physical reality surrounding us from its minimum dimensional level.

We conjecture that the atomic elements of reality are instantiations of MoR, that is they "perceive", "think" and "act" – if this sounds like a sort of physical animism, it will later be clarified that it is not; it is, instead, a necessary consequence of the isomorphism between physical and informational reality we were talking of.

At a superior dimensional level, any natural or artificial system (*system*: here is another notion we will characterize in greater detail later) surrounding us is an aggregate of these elementary entities and, in its turn, it implements models of reference, that is to say, it "perceives", "thinks" and "acts". Specifically, at human functional level, that is, at the level of the system *man*, it is the MoR that explain our actions, on the basis of how we perceive the external world (*internal* and *external* are other notions to be specified in due course).

Hence, MoR have a "fractal" nature, as they are realized in an isomorphic manner at extremely different levels, from electron to man, to the galaxy. Thus, they are ideal candidates to work as a conceptual interface between the physical and informational world.

This introductory outline might have resulted a little puzzling. So let us further explore, still in an informal yet precise manner (we will come to formalizations in the following chapters) our two ideas, isomorphism between physics and information and models of reference, starting with the former.

0.1 The physical universe

0.1.1 Computation everywhere

"There's Plenty of Room at the Bottom" is the significant title of a prophetic conference held in 1959 by Richard Feynman at the California Institute of Technology. Thenceforth, the spectacular development of nanotechnologies has led computer scientists to increasingly focus on the physical implementability of their computational models.

Actually, computation as we know it today could soon be a thing of the past. One of the reasons why today's computers have difficulties in realizing what we call "intelligence" is that they do not capture, if not in a very unsophisticated form, certain aspects – in particular, the "non-logical" ones – typical of human intelligence. But normal computers are sometimes ineffective even in their specific field of competence, namely in performing computations: for example, we can think of the difficulty in factoring very large integers (an essential activity for internet security, cryptograpy, etc.). On the contrary, nanotechnologies and research in non-standard computability theories show that we can find computation (and computation in a precise, not merely intuitive but mathematically respectable sense) where least expected, in the tiniest meanderings of reality: at the biological level, in the way in which DNA, RNA and proteins store and transmit genetic information; at the chemical and physical level, in the distribution and movement of perfect gases; and even in the subatomic reality described by quantum theory. A quantum computer is still an idea, but not an unrealizable one.

Reasearchers at Harvard and Princeton are studying the possibility of building biological computers, actually constituted of DNA, RNA and protein chains, and capable of computing Boolean operators in the organic cells: taking as input ("perceiving", we will learn to say as we progressively develop the theory of the models of reference) material in the cytoplasm, elaborating ("thinking") it, and delivering as output (as their specific "action") molecules easily recognizable in laboratory (we will investigate this issue in one of the appendices to this book, dedicated to biological reality). Other forms of computation exploit the chemical and physical properties of specific materials, such as carbon (this will be dealt with in another appendix to this book: we will see that empirical researches focused on materials of this kind are revealing a substantive covergence with the abstract computational model developed in our laboratory, and introduced in this book).

These forms of computation share some common technical characte-ristics: they work in largely *parallel* fashion; they are able to realize in a single physical support both the *memorization* and the *transfer* of signals; and they can reduce to polynomial problems some computations which, from the standpoint of normal computers, are of exponential complexity. These are all points we will come back to. What concerns us now is the physical and informational outline this situation suggests: perhaps the universe we are part of can veritably be seen as a computer, whose activity at each instant t consists of calculating its own state in the following instant $t+1$ (and in doing so, as we will see, locally and digitally). In this ontological perspective, "information plays the role of a primitive variable which informs the course about the development of the universe"[1] which means that *information* must be numbered as a physical primitive alongside with such notions as *space* and *time*.[2] But how must a universe, such as one that can be *thought* of in these terms, be *made*? Here is our proposal.

0.1.2 A discrete universe

What follows is an informal presentation of our model of physical universe.[3] As we will see in Chapter 3, the model can be formally specified (or better still, axiomatically characterized). However, pursuing the general strategy of this book, we begin with an intuitive explanation, and come back to the concepts later, several times in a series of concentric circles of subsequent in-depth examinations.

We consider that a universe in which information and matter are two different ways of representing a single thing must be *discrete* and *finite*. In particular, at its bottom there must be *minimum space-time units*, not further divisible. This modelling of reality is one Albert Einstein and Erwin Schroedinger held dear; we find it in the recent twistor theory; and it does not contradict any of the presently known physical laws. Specifically, recent theories of quantum gravity affirm that time and space must exactly consist of discrete *quanta*, taken as essentially informational items.

How small are these minimal quantities? If electrons can be found at a dimensional level of the order of 10^{-15} m, on the basis of our current

---

[1] Ilachinski [2001], p. 605. Following Ray Kurzweil we poetically describe ourselves as "patternists", that is, as "somebody who believes that information patterns are the fundamental reality" (Kurzweil [2005], p. 5) – we do not think, though, that "the world is made of stories, not of atoms" (Ibid); as we will see, our digital world is made of stories *and* atoms.

[2] For some illustrous reference, see the *computing universe* theorized by Konrad Zuse [1982], and the monumental Wolfram [2002].

[3] Taken from Canonico and Rossi [2007], Ch. 2 and *passim*.

body of knowledge we might have to move up to 10^{-35} m for minimum spatial units, and perhaps take a range at around 10^{-44} seconds for minimum time units, coherently with the theoretical structure proposed by Max Planck. However this is, of course, of minor importance from a conceptual point of view: what is essential is that the "ultimate atoms" *exist* – that they are out there (and, as we will see, that they behave in a certain way).

We call these atoms cells. We believe the cells can instantiate, at every time t, one of a finite set of *properties*, but we would rather talk of *states*, leaving to the term "property" its broader sense. We expect the states of elementary cells to be quite few, and that all the limitless variety of characteristics, properties and relations exhibited by our world at higher dimensional levels must emerge from those few base levels: from base *configurations* of cells, that is, from the distribution of states within the cells, or within *aggregates* of cells, at a given time – *configuration*, *aggregate*: here are other notions we will investigate later on, and of which we will provide a precise formal characterization.

If anything that exists is, all in all, a more or less vast aggregate of cells, our perspective on the physical world moves from an honest *conventionalism* in the following sense: if we define *system* as any aggregation of contiguous cells within space, then any system exists in the same way as any other; as we will see in Chapter 3 of the book, it is plausible to assume that our cognitive apparatus has led us to systematically take into consideration only those portions of reality which appear interesting to us or cognitively salient – those who "catfy" or those who "personify", for example. But it is us who delineate the boundaries of the things of the world we are interested in – consciously or not.

Furtermore, we believe that the universe does not evolve randomly, but rather according to laws operating from the ultimate level upwards: there exist deterministic rules that set the changes of state of the cells. We do not know with certainty what these rules are (but a substantial part of the sense of this book lies in formulating a couple of hypotheses in this regard); nevertheless, we do know that they can be conceived as specific *models of reference*, that is, sequences of perception-thought-action (to be more precise, you will be able to start seeing them this way, as the notion of MoR is progressively developed). At any time t, the whole universe will have a certain configuration, that is to say, it will be the aggregate of all the atoms or cells, each instantiating the state it happens to have at time t – and it will happen to have a given state in that instant, on the basis of (a) the state it had in the immediately previous time instant, and (b) rules determining the state transitions.[4]

This is the end of our basic description of the universe: all the rest – the whole complexity of the world surrounding us – must descend from this simple sequence of elements: space, time, states, and rules. Let us elaborate them more thoroughly.

0.1.3 Space and time

Let us assume that space is entirely occupied and uniformly subdivided into regular shapes (namely, the cells). In a three-dimensional space, the regular forms into which it can be so subdivided are tetrahedron, cube, and rhombic dodecahedron. The two-dimensional analogues are equilateral triangle, square, and hexagon. As will be made clear from Chapter 1 onwards, the adoption of a two-dimensional model is sufficient to perform several computational simulations able to capture the most diverse properties of the "intended model" we are now describing.

In our laboratory, after numerous experimentations and computer simulations we opted for the rhombic dodecahedron and its two-dimensional analogue, the hexagon. These forms have various topological advantages in the representation of movement and change, and the distance between cells can be approximated in terms of radius. Let us consider the two-dimensional hexagonal case: around a single cell there are six equidistant cells; at distance 2 there exist six other cells with the same angle and the same distance between them, and so on. The fact that the reality of space is so construed implies that, even if the perfect circle and the perfect sphere do not subsist "in reality", they can however be easily approximated:

---

[4] It is worth mentioning that recent physical theories speculate on a multiplicity of universes generated in a regular manner, each with its base rules. However, most universes have a very short life, or do not evolve in any interesting way, because the rules do not allow for the production of interesting *patterns* and increasingly complex forms. On the contrary, our universe has evidently had a fairly prolific endowment. In particular, the rules have produced such structures as human intelligence, which have the unique capacity of being able to investigate those same rules that produced them and govern them. This phenomenon, as we will see, is captured by our mathematical theory in terms of the notion of *recursion*.

···

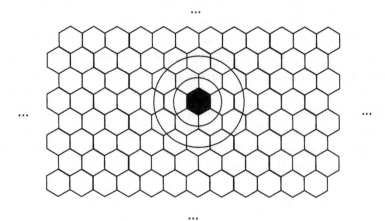

···   ···

···

Our discretist and finitist option, as for space, likewise requires time to have minimum units: the instants. Algebraically, time should be a discrete linear order of instants. A philosophically pregnant question is: does an absolute-uniform time exist or not? As we will see in Chapter 1, there are reasons to uphold absolute time – not only reasons of computational efficiency, but, specifically, reasons of coherence with the discretist option; however this discussion must be postponed with respect to the current, rapid intuitive presentation. It is to be noted that the concept of discrete time and space matches that of a maximum reachable speed, which, according to relativity theory, would be the speed of light; but the former is not dependent on the latter.

We also stress the following, extremely important fact: in a universe like the one we are describing, *motion is always apparent*. What we label as "movement", and we perceive as such at the macro-level is, in fact, a change of state undergone by the cells through time. As a consequence, the (apparent) maximum reachable velocity would be determined by the change of state of two adjacent cells from instant t to instant $t+1$; this is another point we will go back to later on, in Chapter 3, by formally developing such an ontological idea.

0.1.4 States and rules

Establishing the states and rules at the bottom level of the world is a truly hard task for anyone who believes in a discrete universe. It is, of course, a largely conjectural activity, because nobody is (at this moment) in a position to empirically verify what the minimal cells of the world actually "do"! On the other hand, in a seriously reductionist perspective, as was stressed, *everything* should befall, one way or another, on the basic states and rules – all the endless copiousness of the observable universe.

From a theoretical point of view, we believe that the number of states the cells can assume must not only be finite, but also very small, and that the same must hold for the number of rules. Furthermore, for reasons of computational efficiency, the state of each single cell should depend (on the rules and) on the state of the adjacent cells – or better, on the state of the *immediately* adjacent cells, that is to say, in the two-dimensional case, the six cells surrounding each hexagon. What must be held firm is that we do not admit mysterious "actions at a distance". The consequences of these options, again, will be clarified from Chapter 1 onwards, while for the time being this first intuitive and informal description is sufficient. Another tenet of our approach is, as we were anticipating, the deterministic character of the rules: at each instant t, the state of each cell is univocally determined by the state of the cell and that of the relevant cells at $t+1$, and by the rules. The seemingly casual manifestations of the universe are appearances which emerge only at a higher level with respect to the fundamental reality.

On the basis of this first characterization of our universe, we can already begin to understand in what sense speaking of "physical properties of objects", and speaking of "distribution of information", equals having two manners of describing the same thing: to say that everything is hardware (physical, body) is equivalent to saying that everything is software (information, mind). On the one hand, we have a description in terms of states (of the atoms) of the world, on the other, a description in terms of information contents implemented by (groups of) atoms, and of rules that operate on such contents. In our "intended model", each modification of the physical state of matter corresponds to a modification in information content, and vice versa. In a slogan: modulo the digital nature of our model, hardware and software are perfectly interchangeable. This is nothing but a generalization and an accentuation of what we already observe occurring in particular, and extremely important, domains. A software instruction can modify the state of a computer memory (hence, produce changes at the physical level), which will send, let us suppose, a signal to a printer; conversely, a modification in a computer memory can determine an alteration in a program code.

Analogously, one thought of ours modifies the physical state of our brain, which can determine a rational or an emotional answer realized in our body – from the involuntary redding of the face, to an organized and complex sequence of actions such as traversing a crossing, painting a picture, or demonstrating a theorem; and conversely, a physical modifi- cation in our brain changes our thoughts; an alteration in the DNA genetic "software" modifies the organism that will result from the cor- responding physical development.

Now for the key claim: if the universe is, ultimately, entirely constituted in this way, and if – and, *since*, as we will demonstrate in the next Chapter – in such a universe there can be, already at the most elementary level, computers, that is to say, universal Turing machines, namely machines capable of computing all that is computable (on the basis of the Turing- Church Thesis), then in principle it is possible to construct computers with computational capacity of a higher order of magnitude than the present ones. Artificial intelligence is not that "artificial", because it already exists at the very bottom of nature. But what is – this, as we were saying, is the other problem of AI – "intelligence"? It is here that the models of reference, which are the actual central characters of this book, come into the picture.

0.2 Our first approach to MoR

Let us therefore come to our second basic idea: the models of refer- ence. A MoR, as we have said, is a deterministic and temporally ordered sequence <perception → thought → action>. Another way to conceive the MoR is to think of them as mechanisms that, starting from stimuli, produce actions. The idea in itself is not original at all. What is perhaps innovative and certainly striking is to consider the MoR to be at the bottom of the functioning of our mind and, indeed, of that of any living being. If you are able to read this page, we dare say, is thanks to the activation of the relevant MoR. If we understand (misunderstand) each other in communication, it is because we are endowed (not endowed) with specific shared MoR. And moreover MoR have, we were claiming, a "fractal" nature: they are active in your eye in order to enable it to process visual stimuli and send certain signals to your cerebral area devoted to vision; it is by means of appropriate MoR that a frog can catch a fly in front of it with its tongue; and it is, again, through the relevant MoR that at the signal "green light" we put our car into gear, we set it in motion, and we traverse a crossing. Contrariwise, we are phobic because our mind activates an "erroneous" series of MoR; we develop tumors because the "wrong" MoR are hard-pressed by certain cells; we vote for a particular political party on the basis of a series of MoR; and so on. But also an arithmetic operation (as we will examine in Chapter 4 of this volume), or a business software, or a mathematical theorem can be explained in terms of MoR.

If that is how things stand, this leaves open the possibility that all our thoughts could be mathematically tractable, and, in particular, describable, in a formal and computationally characterizable language. It is a controversial question whether our thoughts can be formalized in a model like the "intended model" we began introducing, and even more, what such model is, if there is one. From our point of view, what is essential is the usefulness of the model itself, i.e., its applicability in practice.

On the other hand, there are plausible indications in the direction we pursue: any decision of ours seems to be determined by a number (large, but on the basis of our assumptions, finite) of concurrent factors. These factors can potentially be identified and measured. Therefore, in principle it is always possible to progress towards the knowledge of how much each factor affects our actions – and even "irrational" variables intervening in the relevant decisions, such as the tone of voice of the shop assistant, or the way articles are displayed, in the action of purchasing a good, reveal themselves as effectively measurable.

If by "mind" we mean the procedures that allow our brain to function, then such procedures *shall be* models of reference, that is, deterministic sequences of instructions, "activated" by perceptions or inputs, and which manipulate (that is to say, from a mental point of view, "think") these inputs, providing us with corresponding actions.

And such sequences have precise physical *realizers*. A substantial part of our book is devoted to an abstract mathematical treatment of the MoR.

But, as we have already noticed and as we will further examine in the appendices of the volume, it is easy to recognize how they are realized in the biological world of the cells, in the physico-chemical one of nano-technological materials, and even in the socio-economic reality.

We believe that our brain – the most interesting portion of physical reality known to us – implements a vast number of MoR, in part innate and in part acquired through experience. Variously combined with each other (in mathematically precise ways, as we will see in what follows), these MoR determine all of our perceptions, thoughts, and actions. MoR must be activated by conformations of signals coming via our (internal and external) sense organs as inputs, which univocally and deterministi-cally initiate their execution. And this process must occur at all cognitive levels, whether conscious or not. There must be both innate MoR en-coded in the DNA, and instructions realized in the genes, determining the implementability of the MoR in the brain. Some of these MoR will have to be dedicated to the production of new MoR, which in turn are memorized in the respective nervous systems thereby becoming part of the regular cognitive and behavioural process.

By now our first informal description of MoR should lead our reader to understand why, if such hypothesis holds, it will enable us to treat in a mathematically adequate manner also aspects of our mind that so far have appeared inaccessible to a computational approach. In the next chapter, we will begin to formally develop the mathematics of the MoR presenting how, starting from a tiny number of fundamental MoR, implemented in a definite manner in the atoms or cells of the *physical* universe we are initially delineating, we can configure a *computational* universe in which *all* that is susceptible of being computationally treated, can be effectively derived. Let us take off!

1. Universal Computation

In this chapter we show that a universe like the one informally described in the introduction of this book can encompass computation: *if* the universe is such, *then* universal computation is embedded in its ultimate and most elementary dimensional level, and the isomorphism between matter and information we hold dear is most properly vindicated.

Demonstrating that this is how things work is not straightforward at all. It is a notorious fact that not all the physical constraints on computation are captured by traditional computational models (for instance, by the regular current representations of what a Turing machine is; but also by the sequential structure of the ordinary von Neumann computers existing nowadays). In particular, such a missing constraint is *reversibility*: the dynamic laws of physics are reversible at microscopic and deterministic level, implying that distinct initial states in the evolution of a microphysical system always lead to distinct final states (and this is valid both for the classical formulation of the laws, and for that in terms of quantum mechanics). As a consequence, anyone willing to simulate the real computational procedures at the root of the nature of the basic entities that compose our physical universe, should resort to reversible dynamic rules (and moreover, rules that maintain certain additive quantities) – that is to say, in our perspective, to *models of reference*.

The model we propose here is a *cellular automaton* displaying a perfectly reversible dynamics, and capable of storing the totality of the information from the beginning of the universe. We will demonstrate, in a mathematically rigorous way, that our physical-informational universe realizes the Boolean logical operators and the other building blocks of universal computation. Consequently, in our digital world it is possible to develop and have computers, that is, universal Turing machines, capable of computing (if we accept the Church-Turing Thesis) anything that is computable.

All this stems from a unique rule that, as we will see, incorporates in fact two primitive operators or MoR as its sub-rules. This double rule is in turn a model of reference in all respects, on the basis of the characterization of MoR designed in the introduction; it is directly implemented in *each* of the cells of our universe; and it is a MoR that can function as "computational primitive" from which anything that is computable can be derived, as we will analyse in the following chapters – in particular, in Chapter 4, devoted to recursive MoR.

Hence, our model stands as a candidate to provide significant indications for the realization of high performance computational systems: systems that use the resources offered by the physical world in the most efficient way – for instance, by showing how logical circuits with virtually null internal energy dissipation can be built. We will see in an appendix of this volume that there are, as mentioned above, considerable convergences between our theoretical model and some recent progresses in the field of nanotechnology. In our opinion, the interaction between abstract computational models and their realization in nanomaterials is the main path to accomplish the computational optimization of the world – to achieve what futurist Ray Kurzweil has defined "saturation with intelligence" of the matter: "The use of *patterns* of matter and energy in the optimal way, on the basis of our comprehension of the physics of computation".[5]

1.1 The theory of cellular automata: towards a "physics of thought"

Cellular automata (CA) are mathematical representations of *complex systems* – that is, of dynamic systems composed of a plurality of parts interacting nonlinearly. CA are the object of numerous studies by researchers for various reasons: firstly, they allow to represent and simulate the development of a great variety of dynamic structrures – from neural networks, to genetic algorithms that translate the evolution of life in a computationally tractable form, to certain chemical reactions, up to complex socio-economic and military systems.

---

[5] Kurzweil [2005], p. 29.

Secondly, they are useful conceptual models to study in an extremely pure form the development of *patterns*: a salient feature of CA lies in the fact that complex phenomena emerge, at high level, as a result of the cooperation among simple individuals that, at low level, act and interact on the basis of elementary rules. Probably, *the* complex system *par excellence* is composed of the most fascinating portion of physical world we know: the human brain, in which $\sim 10^{10}$ neurons, variously interconnected and operating under precise biochemical rules, produce that aggregate of capacities we group under the term "intelligence"

But there is a third reason to deal with CA, and that is what we most prize in this work: the fact that CA can found a computational *physics*; they can provide a computational model of the physical reality surrounding us. The hallmark of cellular automata is in fact their discrete, besides deterministic, nature. In the model we developed we have also wanted to preserve the basic intuition of *finitism* we mentioned in the Introduction: no part of the theory shall have to make use – to put it in philosophical terms – of the notion of actual, as opposed to potential, infinity. Our strategy conforms to what Edward Fredkin has named Finite Nature Hypothesis:

> Finite Nature is the hypothesis that ultimately every quantity of physics, including space and time, will turn out to be discrete and finite; that the amount of information in any small volume of space-time will be finite and equal to one of a small number of possibilities. [...] Finite Nature implies that the basic substrate of physics operates in a manner similar to the workings of certain specialized computers called Cellular Automata. [...] Finite nature does not just hint that the informational aspects of physics are important, it insists that the informational aspects are all there is to physics at the most microscopic level.[6]

1.2 Digital universe

We start by specifying in a mathematically precise manner the model of "digital universe" (call it **U**) we developed and informally explained in the introduction. In our research laboratory we have created a simple software, which exactly realizes the model of universe we are going to

---

[6] Fredkin [1993].

describe:

1) Discrete space-time: any CA consists of a grid of elementary cells. This grid can be one-, two-, three-, or multi-dimensional. The model we have chosen is the two-dimensional one – a solution that concurrently allows (a) to model real physical phenomena, and (b) to preserve the intuitivity of the mereotopological structure.

We know from the introduction that a single cell can be taken as the elementary unit of space. Furthermore, in conformity with our finitist assumption, this space must be finite: there exists at most a finite, albeit large, number, say w, of cells, that is, of minimum spatial units (even though the CA studied in the literature are mostly built upon infinite spaces, the finitistic restriction nevertheless comes into play when these are computer modelled, given the necessarily finite nature of the memory of any calculator). Moreover, also time is discrete and formed by minimum units: the instants, $t_0, t_1 \ldots$

2) Homogeneity of the gird: all cells are equivalent from a morphological point of view. The larger part of the scientists who study CA choose the square (let us think for example of the historic Conway's *Life*), but we have favored, as we were saying, the hexagon:

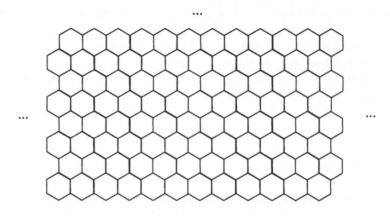

It is however to be borne in mind that the computational results attainable with the CA we realized equally apply to a classical square grid (thanks to the specific characteristics of the rule which determines the evolution of the universe, and that we will expose here). Once a spatial basis has been fixed, in a two-dimensional context each cell is univocally individuated spatially by an ordered couple of integers $<i, j>$: the grid references of its position in the two-dimensional space. As we will see within two chapters, also the mereotopological structure of the universe **U** can be defined in a completely satisfying manner, through a *purely axiomatic* characterization.

If the universe is finite, what are its "borders"? And won't there however be something beyond any (presumed) limit of the universe? This ancient paradox burdened onto finitists in a sense also concerns those who assume models with an infinity of cells, since, as we mentioned, any computer simulation of a CA can implement at most a finite number of cells. A solution often employed consists in setting periodic limits; for instance a two-dimensional grid with w cells can be spread on a torus, thereby establishing if the w-th cell is $<m, n>$, that $<m, n+1> = <m, 0>$ and $<m+1, n> = <0, n>$. Alternatively, the borders that encompass a w-cell universe are often arbitrarily stipulated as instantiating one single designated state, so that they are not affected by the computation occurring inside the universe. Any standard configuration will, however, suit – for our purposes, this makes little difference.

3) Discrete states: we know that, at each instant of time t, each cell $<i, j>$ finds itself in one and only one state $\sigma \in \Sigma$, where Σ is a finite set of discrete states of cardinality $|\Sigma| = k$. We will denote by "$\sigma_{i, j, t}$" the state of the cell $<i, j>$ at time t.

4) Local Interactions: in the introduction, we declared that mysterious "actions at a distance" are not contemplated in our universe. Specifically, we establish that each cell $<i, j>$ only interacts with the six adjacent cells – its *neighbourhood* – that we can conventionally number from 1 to 6 counterclockwise, in this manner:

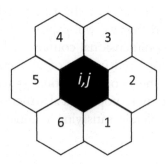

We will denominate by "$[i, j]$" the neighbourhood of cell $<i, j>$.

5) Dynamic rule: at each discrete unit of time, each cell $<i, j>$ updates its state with respect to the immediately previous instant on the basis of a single rule, that is, of a single MoR, taking into account the states of the cells in its neighbourhood. In order to present the rule, we start by introducing a very simple functional notation, which we will return to in detail later on, and with which we can formalize in a precise manner the functioning of *any* MoR.

1.3 Functional notation for the MoR

We claimed that any MoR is a deterministic operator, which univocally associates to certain inputs or perceptions some outputs or actions, as a consequence of internal elaborations or thoughts. Then, it will certainly make sense to state that each MoR is associated with the correspondent of the *domain* of an operator, and with the correspondent of the *codomain* of an operator. We can now provide the following characterization.

The domain (let it be A) of any MoR is the totality of its possible perceptions, namely the inputs upon which the MoR is defined. Intuitively, not every MoR can accept any perception as input: for example, the MoR **traversing a crossing (only) on a green light**[7] takes as input something like "perception green light", not something like "cheese sandwich" (which obviously does not exclude, in an openly conventio-

---

[7] Henceforth we will write the expressions that designate, in ordinary informal language, a model of reference in **boldface**.

nalist perspective such as ours, that there exist conventions for which
"cheese sandwich" can be seen as a signal meaning "green light"!). And,
again intuitively, not every MoR can give any action as output, but only
actions of a certain type: thus **traversing a crossing (only) on a green
light** will trigger, on the perception "green light", a series of acts performed by the driver as action or output, not "grabbing a byte of sandwich" (again: without ruling out conventions according to which
"grabbing a byte of sandwich" can be seen as a signal meaning "push the
clutch/put into gear...", etc).

The codomain (say, B) of a MoR is the totality of possible actions, that
is, the outputs the MoR can give with respect to the inputs or perceptions upon which it is defined. Let us consider, then, a model of reference f, which has A as the entirety of the perceptions upon which it is
defined, and B as the totality of the associable actions. We will write:

$$f(x_1, x_2, ..., x_n) = y$$

where the variables x_1, x_2, ... x_n vary on the perceptions admissible in
A, and the variable y varies on actions admissible in B (strictly speaking ,
we could write:

$$f(<x_1, x_2, ..., x_n>) = y$$

to highlight that the order of succession of the components of a structured input is relevant, hence, in theory, the inputs form an n-tuple.
However, in the remainder of this book this will sometimes be taken for
granted to simplify the notation).[8]

We can adopt an operational notation and write:

$$f: A \Rightarrow B$$

---

[8] Besides, we observe that the general operational notation admits interesting specifications. In
particular, the domain of definition of y can in turn be structured – abiding by the univocal and
deterministic character of the transformation of input into output by *each* MoR. MoR can
transform structured pluralities (ordered n-tuples, vector spaces, etc.): we will already analyse an
example with the super rule, discussed *infra*, which is a transformation of informational structures
that can be expressed as sextuples into other informational structures. The qualification of the
form of the MoR can thus be correspondingly more expressive, for instance with schemes of the
type: $f(<x_1, x_2, x_3, x_4, x_5, x_6>) = g(<x_1, x_2, x_3, x_4, x_5, x_6>)$, etc.

to mean "the model of reference f from A to B", where A are exactly the perceptions the model can receive as input, and B are the actions that f can deliver after having elaborated its thoughts.

Given this formal notation, the rule or MoR we seek – let us say $\phi: \Sigma \Rightarrow \Sigma$ is a deterministic operator from states to states.[9] The state of a cell $<i, j>$ at $t+1$ is entirely determined (in a way we will examine shortly) by the states of the neighbourhood $[i, j]$ at t on the basis of ϕ:

$$\sigma_{i, j, t+1} = \phi(\sigma_{[i, j], t})$$

Our universe works in a *homogeneous* way, not only in the sense that the cells are morphologically equivalent, but also inasmuch as they are all governed by the unique operator or rule ϕ. There exist non-homogeneous cellular automata, namely ones in which different cells can be governed by distinct rules that determine the respective state transitions. The possibility to implement multiple rules facilitates the attainement of many computational results (for example: emulating a universal Turing machine within the CA in question).[10] We nevertheless believe that a homogeneous arrangement with a single rule has a superior elegance, most of all when (as we will see below) it allows to achieve the same computational results of a non-homogeneous one. Obviously, *detecting* a single rule that alone does all that could be done with a multiplicity of rules has not been an easy task at all. On the contrary, it required prolonged research to our laboratory. On the other hand, there are sound theoretical reasons beyond elegance to commit to the single rule. First of all, a multiple rule solution may fall into a *slippery slope* insofar as the exact number of rules is concerned (why three and not four or five or ... ?); secondly, the quality of a rootedness of (universal) computation into the ultimate reality of the universe lies in the possibility to let computational rules (and ontological patterns as well) *emerge* from simplicity; and nothing is simpler than unity over multiplicity, that is, possibly, the idea that if there are many rules or MoR, they must emerge from a basic

---

[9] Normally, a rule ρ for a CA is a function from n-tuples of states to states, that is $\rho: \Sigma^n \to \Sigma$, where n is the number of cells constituting the neighbourhood. However, we will see that our MoR-super rule ϕ is directly a function from single inputs that *are* n-tuples (in particolar, sextuples), to n-tuples (sextuples), in consideration of the particolar topological structure of our neighbourhood. Such characteristic is functional to the reversibility of ϕ, that, as we will see, is one of its crucial qualities.

[10] See Sipper [2004].

operational unit.

1.4 The four characteristics of the universe

We claimed in the Introduction that our universe should work, according to our theoretical options, in a *synchronous* manner: each point in the net, that is to say, each of the atomic cells, simultaneously updates its state. Such arrangement is widely prevalent in most studies on CA; although some have explored the option of asynchronous universes,[11] there are independent reasons in support of the synchronous option: if we accept the hypothesis of absolute time, synchronicity is consistent with our finitary and discrete base assumption. In fact if distinct cells update their state at different but commensurable times, then asynchronicity is, in a way, only apparent. But if times are incommensurable with each other, their ratio is an irrational number, which introduces an element that is incompatible with our assumption that everything, at the ultimate and fundamental levels of reality, is discrete and enumerable.

Our model of universe therefore has three conceptual characteristics that are typical of every CA:

1) Information is locally (at the single cell level) **and globally** (at the level of the universe as a whole) **finite.** Each portion of space encompasses and processes a finite quantity of information; and the same holds for the universe as a whole. If we call *configuration* of our universe $\mathbf{U}$ at time t the overall state of $\mathbf{U}$ at that time, we can express a configuration in a vector notation: the configuration of the universe at time t, $\overline{\sigma}_t$ is nothing but the ordered sequence of the states of each cell of the universe at t, that is $\overline{\sigma}_t = <\sigma_{0,0,t}, \sigma_{0,1,t}, \sigma_{1,0,t}, \sigma_{1,1,t}, \sigma_{1,2,t}, \cdots, \sigma_{i,j,t}, \cdots, \sigma_{m,n,t}> \in \Gamma$, where Γ is the whole spectrum of configurations (*phase space*).

Since each cell can take one of a finite number of states $|\Sigma| = k$, and there exists a finite number w of cells in the universe, there will be at most k^w possible configurations. As a consequence, the entire evolution

---

[11] See Ingerson and Buvel [1984].

of the universe **U** is represented by a finite *transition graph* G_Φ, which is the graph defined by the global transition rule $\Phi: \Gamma \Rightarrow \Gamma$, the function induced by our local MoR-rule ϕ, which maps configurations to configurations:

$$\sigma_{t+1} = \Phi(\ \overline{\sigma_t})$$

The finiteness of our universe, and in particular of the graph G implies that, whatever its initial configuration, its evolution will have to exhibit a periodic cycle after at most k^w iterations of the rule governing it.

2) Information is locally processed: as in our universe action at a distance is ruled out, possible *apparent* "actions at a distance"[12] are to be considered as approximations emerging at higher dimensional levels, because state transitions are local in time and space: each cell in the lattice interacts only with its neighbourhood, and its state at instant t totally depends on what occurs (in the neighbourhood) at the immediately previous instant.

3) Information is processed *in parallel*: what happens at the ultimate level of reality is that a huge number of cells process their own states according to the connections to the respective neighbourhood.

Our universe shares these three characteristics, as we have claimed, with many other systems of cellular automata. But it possesses a fourth feature, which singles it out with respect to the majority of the known systems (for instance, Conway's *Life*):

4) Information is *entirely preserved*: this is due to the fact that the (single) rule or MoR on the basis of which our entire universe evolves at the ultimate level is strongly *reversible (time-reversal invariant)*. In order to illustrate the import of this point,

a. we will start by explaining what it means that a rule (or, generally, any MoR) is *reversibile*, distinguishing two senses of reversibility − a weak sense and a strong one;

---

[12] Including those of quantum physics, such as per the nonlocality implied by the famous thought experiment by Einstein, Podolski and Rosen [1935].

b. we will then formulate in exact mathematical terms our fundamental rule-MoR ϕ;

c. After establishing that our rule is strongly reversibile, we will explain why this fact is of cardinal importance, both as far as the physical realizability of the model our universe consists in is concerned, and in terms of the computational efficiency of the model itself.

1.5 Weak and strong reversibility of MoR

The vast majority of the rules governing the dynamics of well-known CA are irreversibile. In order to clearly understand what we are dealing with, we begin by noticing that the (ir)reversibility of any MoR is completely analogous to that of any mathematical function which is (not) one-to-one and onto: a MoR is said to be *irreversible* when different inputs or perceptions can give rise to the same output or action. Correspondingly, in a cellular automaton a global rule P (that is a map from configurations to configurations) is defined irreversibile when different configurations of the system at t can lead to the same configuration at $t+1$. When this occurs – and it does occur in the great majority of cases: the rule of Conway's *Life* is not invertible, but also the simplest boolean functions, such as AND and OR, are not so – it is generally not possible, by only looking at the configuration of an automaton at time $t+1$, to establish what was its configuration at t.

By contrast, a rule ρ: A $\Rightarrow$ B for a CA is said to be (weakly) reversibile when it has an inverse ρ^{-1}: B $\Rightarrow$ A. Naturally – again, in standard functional notation – ρ^{-1} is the inverse of ρ if and only if $\rho^{-1} \circ \rho = Id_A$: A $\Rightarrow$ A (and $\rho \circ \rho^{-1} = Id_B$: B $\Rightarrow$ B), where Id is the identity function, and $\circ$ is the composition operator; hence, $(\rho^{-1} \circ \rho)(\sigma_{i,j,t}) = \rho^{-1}(\rho(\sigma_{i,j,t})) = \sigma_{i,j,t}$.

The same goes for the global rule P: $\Gamma \Rightarrow \Gamma$, that is the map from configurations to configurations of the CA which is induced by the corresponding local rule. The invertibility of P ensures that each overall state $\overline{\sigma} \in \Gamma$ of the universe has exactly one predecessor $\overline{\sigma}^1 \in \Gamma$, such that P($\overline{\sigma}^1$) = $\overline{\sigma}$.

The property of a rule (and therefore, of a MoR) of being reversibile means that there exists an inverse operator or MoR which transforms the output of the former into the respective input. If, given a rule, we can find its inverse, then, in principle, we are able to run a CA "in reverse" and to retrieve its previous configurations. Hence, the only reversible rules are those corresponding to functions that are one-to-one and onto (save, of course, the fact that injective functions are invertible on their image, which is a subset of the respective codomain).

A rule ρ (and thus, again, a MoR) is said to be *strongly reversibile* (or *time-reversal invariant*)[13] when it is the inverse of itself, that is $\rho^{-1} = \rho$. Obviously, this is a stronger property than the previous one: when a rule is strongly reversible, the sequence of past states of the CA can be recovered by simply inverting time (that is to say, with a transformation that inverts: $t \mid\rightarrow -t$), and letting the CA compute its states according to its rule. The same initial configuration of the universe can be restored through an evolution in reverse based on the same rule that governed it when time was running forward, as if we ran film frames in reverse.

1.6 Super-rule: the fundamental MoR

It is clear why the vast majority of the dynamic rules governing CA are not reversible: save the case of the "solipsistic" neighbourhood, in which each cell is (trivially) neighbour solely to itself, the set of states that constitute the neighbourhood of a cell (let us consider the cell identified by $<i, j>$) at a time t generally can't be retrieved by looking only at the state of $<i, j>$ at $t+1$. To obtain a local rule giving rise to a globally reversibile CA we therefore need to proceed very carefully.

In our model we started by assuming that the state of each cell in the grid is not a single bit, but rather a *sextuple* of bits, corresponding to the six sides of the cell itself:

---

[13] See Ilachinski [2001], pp. 95, 370.

Each side can assume the value of 1 ("active") or 0 ("inactive"). The state of the cell $<i, j>$ at time t therefore is $\sigma_{i, j, t} = <x_1, x_2, x_3, x_4, x_5, x_6>$, where x_1 corrisponds to side n. 1, x_2 to side n. 2, etc., and each x has value $v \in V = \{1, 0\}$. Since $|V| = 2$, each cell will thus have $2^6 = 64$ instantiable states (that is, $|\Sigma| = 64$).

We define the relevant neighbourhood $[i, j]$ for our cell in a rather original manner. In fact we recall that the general form of the rule-MoR we are seeking is $\sigma_{i, j, t+1} = \phi(\sigma_{[i, j], t})$; but we indicate that each cell assumes as a part of the relevant input for the execution of our dynamic rule ϕ only the value $v \in V$ of the *neighbouring* side of each of the adjacent cells. Hence we can enumerate these sides in the same way:

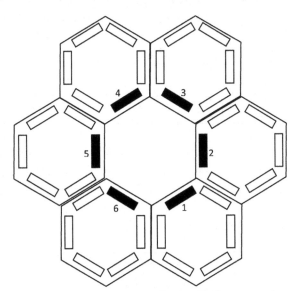

Our rule-MoR, thus, is an operator from single sextuples to single sextuples, that is to say, $\phi: \{1, 0\}^6 \Rightarrow \{1, 0\}^6$. In conformity with the terminology we have been using since the introduction with respect to the MoR, we can think of the dynamics in question as a situation in which each atom or cell *perceives* or reads the output presented to it by the adjacent cells in the respective neighbouring side, and *acts* exposing its own, *thought*, namely computed, output to the neighbours according to the MoR or operator ϕ. Finally, such operator is the following:

$$\sigma_{i,j,\,t+1} = \begin{cases} \text{(a) } Perm(\sigma_{[i,j],\,t}), \text{ if } \sum_{v[i,j],\,t} (\text{mod } 2) = 1 \\ \\ \\ \text{(b) } Id(\sigma_{[i,j],\,t}), \text{ if } \sum_{v[i,j],\,t} (\text{mod } 2) = 0 \end{cases}$$

Where "$\sum_{v[i,j],\,t}$ (mod 2)" denotes the sum modulo 2 of the values $v \in \{1, 0\}$ of each member of the sextuple taken as input at time t.

Id is simply a MoR we can characterize as an identity operator (it is to be borne in mind that we use italic boldface for "ordinary" names, that is, names written in ordinary English, which are assigned to various MoR) defined on Σ, specifically an operator sending each sextuple $\sigma \in \Sigma$ into itself: $Id(<x_1, x_2, x_3, x_4, x_5, x_6>) = <x_1, x_2, x_3, x_4, x_5, x_6>$, that is:

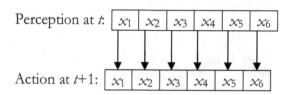

Perm is instead a permutation operator or MoR, which expressly realizes a permutation defined on Σ, that is to say an operator *Perm*: $\Sigma \Rightarrow \Sigma$ which permutes the elements of each sextuple by exchanging the first three items with the last three and vice versa: $Perm(<x_1, x_2, x_3, x_4, x_5, x_6>) = <x_4, x_5, x_6, x_1, x_2, x_3>$, that is:

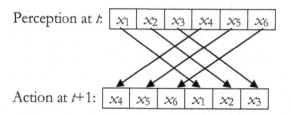

a) If the number of 1s, or of "active bits", of the sextuple perceived in any cell $<i, j>$ is odd (hence, their sum modulo 2 = 1), the cell will give the corresponding permutation as action. As a result, the signal arriving from a cell which is adjacent to $<i, j>$ will be transmitted to the opposite side (let us keep in mind that even if we speak of "opposite sides" and make use of images to stimulate intuition, the spatial directions in our universe are numerically encoded in the order of the members of the sextuples composing the states of each cell – hence it all could easily be mathematically expressed in mereotopological terms: we will formally examine the mereotopological framework in question in a couple of chapters).

For instance, let us determine to blacken a side of each cell if the value of such side is $v = 1$, oppositely leaving it white if $v = 0$. Thus, let us consider the simplest case: that of a single bit 1, perceived by $<i, j>$ in the adjacent cell (let it be $<g, h>$) in the top left corner at time t, while all the other sides are zeros:

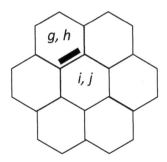

From a computational point of view, what really occurs is that the cell receives in input a well-defined sextuple $[i, j]$ from the cells in the neighbourhood: "a single 1 arriving from the top left" simply means $[i, j] =$ $<0, 0, 0, 1, 0, 0>$ (or, for brevity's sake: 000100). Since, according to our rule, the corresponding output at $t+1$ is $Perm(<0, 0, 0, 1, 0, 0>) = <1, 0, 0, 0, 0, 0>$ (or, for brevity's sake: $Perm(000100) = 100000$), at $t+1$ our cell will exhibit, as its own action, this configuration to the neighbours:

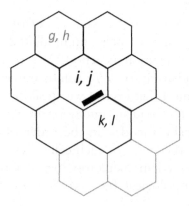

Now let us suppose that the highlighted cell $<k, l>$ finds itself in the same situation in which $<i, j>$ was at the previous instant, that is, it has as the only "active" bit of its neighbourhood the bit exposed to it at $t+1$ by $<i, j>$, namely $[k, l] = 000100$. Also $<k, l>$ will apply *Perm* and at $t+2$ we will have:

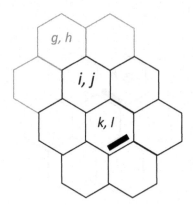

The overall effect will be a "uniform rectilinear motion" of the active bit from the top left to the bottom right (we stress that the term "motion" is simply a way to describe what, in all respects, is a change of state undergone by the cells across time):

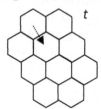

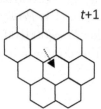

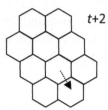

In general, the same will occur any time the input gives an odd number of active bits. For instance, here are three active bits arriving to $<i, j>$ from the directions 2, 3 and 4:

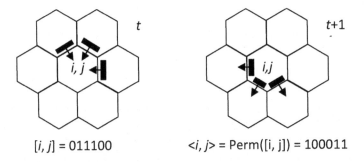

$[i, j]$ = 011100 $<i, j>$ = Perm($[i, j]$) = 100011

b) What happens when the sum of the values of the members of the sextuples is even (and therefore, *Id* applies), is a "kickback" of the signals that are sent back in the directions they came from. For instance, here are two active bits arriving to $<i, j>$ from the directions 2 and 4:

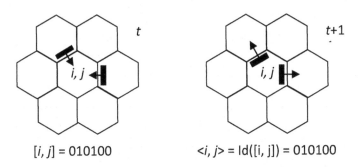

$[i, j]$ = 010100 $<i, j>$ = Id($[i, j]$) = 010100

Finally, we have to bear in mind that, although we focus on the "active" bits, what all the cells do is to compute on the basis of *all* the bits composing the respective states (a perceived input of 010100 will effectively produce an output or action 010100, in which both the two bits = 1 and the four bits = 0 are bounced back).

1.7 Properties of the super-rule

Our fundamental rule or MoR therefore is conceptually straightforward. It operates as a pure conditional routing of signals: it states that if the sum (modulo 2) of the members of the input is even that is = 0, then the signals can proceed in "uniform rectilinear motion", whereas if the sum (modulo 2) is odd, namely = 1, then the signals have to "go back where they came from". Yet, such a MoR gives rise to significant results.

We start by examining some of its simple mathematical features. In the literature on CA the rules in which the state of the cell i at $t+1$ is a function of the sum of the states of the neighbourhood of i at t, excluding i itself, are called *outer-totalistic*. Now our rule-MoR properly matches single n-tuples with single n-tuples; but it can be qualified as outer-totalistic in the sense that the n-tuple exposed by the single cell as output is a function of the sum (modulo 2) of the members of the n-tuples perceived in input by the adjacent cells. Furthermore, (1) our rule-MoR ensures a *total conservation of the number of "active" and "inactive" bits that are present in the universe*: as both *Perm* and (trivially) *Id* are permutations, whatever the perceived sextuple, the corresponding action will always maintain the same number of 1s and 0s.

(2) Besides being conservative, our rule is clearly a reversible MoR, on the grounds of the definition outlined above: in fact, not only the number of "active" and "inactive" bits is retained by it, but each perception is mapped both by *Id* and by *Perm* onto a distinct action.

(3) Finally, our rule is also *strongly* reversible, because it coincides with its inverse, onto which it is mapped by the time reversal transformation: $t \mapsto -t$. Obviously, *Id* is strongly reversible; but *Perm* is strongly reversible as well: given any sextuple $<a, b, c, d, e, f>$ as perception, not only it will be mapped onto a distinct action $<d, e, f, a, b, c>$; but additionally, the rule to go back from the output $<d, e, f, a, b, c>$ to its (only) input is again $Perm(<d, e, f, a, b, c>) = <a, b, c, d, e, f>$.

The fact that our rule ϕ is (strongly) reversible means that in the corresponding global graph, G_ϕ, no so-called *garden-of-eden* emerges, that is, no configuration can only appear as initial configuration, but can never be produced by the evolution of the universe. In fact the combined results provided by Moore e Myhill [1963] show that there exist configurations which do not have any predecessors if and only if there are some with more than one predecessor, which is ruled out by reversibility.

1.8 Reversibility and the physics of information

What inevitably occurs in a non-reversible dynamics is a certain degree of *informational entropy*: the application of an irreversible dynamic rule ρ in a CA can erase a certain quantity of information concerning the past of the system. This is unavoidable, for instance, when a given logic gate has more inputs than outputs: an AND produces a 0; what were the incoming bits? 1 and 0, or 0 and 1, or two zeros?

Up to the 1970s the interest in CA endowed with reversibile rules had been quite scarce, for they were deemed uncapable of supporting universal computation – that is, of the feature, proper of a universal Turing machine (UTM), of evaluating any computable function.[14] Now, although the conservation of information implied by reversibility is certainly a positive fact, without universality not much interesting occurs from the standpoint of computer science. However, in 1973 Charles Bennett demonstrated that universal computation does not necessarily have to be realized through irreversibile logic gates, and in 1976 Toffoli produced the first reversibile CA capable of universal computation, eliciting an interest in this type of models which still persists to this day.

There are at least two reasons – widely stressed in the literature – for which any irreversibile computation is unsatisfactory from a theoretical point of view. The first, more technical one is that irreversible computation is costly: since the time of von Neumann it is known that the cancellation of a bit of information entails an energy cost (at least $\sim 3 \cdot 10^{-21}$ joules at room temperature). The loss of information has a thermodynamic cost, which is paid in terms of a dispersion of "non-computational" energy: the bit of information is lost in the environment, thereby increasing its entropy. Such waste, therefore, is not due to an inefficiency in logic circuit *design*, but it rather has a more fundamental root: it is a direct consequence of the existence of irreversible logic computations. As technology advances, the problem of this energy waste, and the need to build reversible computers with virtually zero

---

[14] It has been proven by Kari [1990] that for a CA on a two- or multi- dimensional grid there does not exist a decision procedure to ascertain, given a CA with a local rule ρ, whether the corresponding configurations-to-configurations global map P is reversible; which is summed up by saying that reversibility of CA for dimensions $d \geq 2$ is undecidable.

energy dissipation, are bound to become increasingly urgent.[15]

The second reason – the one we are most interested in here – is that any irreversibile computation can only mirror a macroscopic physical reality, which is very far from the ultimate ontological level, inasmuch as the dynamic laws of physics are reversibile at microscopic and deterministic level. Vice versa, insofar as the relevant isomorphism is preserved in our model, this stands as a good candidate to provide valuable indications for the realization of high performance computational systems: systems, as we illustrated, which use the resources supplied by the physical world in the most efficient manner.

1.9 Universal computation

Despite its simplicity, our rule-MoR ϕ has something which renders it truly remarkable: in fact it allows our universe **U** to host *computers*: it permits the existence of universal Turing machines (UTMs), capable of computing (if we accept the Church-Turing Thesis) all that is computable. When a rule for a CA allows to do so, it is said to be computation-universal, capable of universal computation. Our rule ϕ, hence, is *computation-universal*.

Obviously, this has to be proven. In the literature there are two essential approaches to demonstrate that a given rule for CA is capable of universal computation: one consists in mathematically reducing such rule to another which is already known to be computation-universal. Another, more "constructive" method, fundamentally involves showing in a direct way that all of the basic building blocks of a conventional computer or of a UTM can be emulated by *patterns* generated by the rule in its domain of action. This is the strategy adopted by Berkelamp, Conway e Guy [1982] in their original demonstration of the fact that *Life* is capable

---

[15] It is fair to say that the idea that reversible computation, unlike its irreversible mate, is safe and sane with respect to energy dissipation, is controversial: see e.g. Shenker [2000], Maroney [2005], for objections to the so-called Landauer Dissipation Thesis that irreversible computation entails irreversible thermodynamic cost as a foundation of a strong connection between information processing and physics. But see also Groisman et al. [2007] for a confirmation of the Thesis via a "phenomenological" argument: they provide a general proof that resetting is a thermodynamic cost independently of the particular model of the physical process of resetting under consideration.

of universal computation, and it is the strategy we will maintain with our CA.

In order for a CA to be computation-universal, in general, it must be able to host configurations of the cells which compose it, such that these can be seen as *patterns* that are stable in time: localized packs of information transportable throughout the lattice. More precisely, the "primitives" of computation include the possibility of (1) *transmitting* and (2) *storing* signals, which require a memory and transmission channels for bits and bit sequences (through which these can flow or be redirectioned, sent out in multiple copies, etc.), as well as (3) the possibility of *processing* the signals, which necessitates of a set of logic gates (such as AND, OR and NOT) that must be functionally complete. Once demonstrated that a CA is capable of containing all these basic building blocks, the actual construction of circuits corresponding to those of a conventional computer is a routine matter, perhaps tedious to complete, but conceptually secondary.

Let us now show how our universe, with its simple reversible rule-MoR, realizes universal computation. First of all, as Edward Fredkin and Tommaso Toffoli showed in their classic *Conservative Logic*, the aforementioned points (1) and (2) are conceptually realized by a single primitive in any reversible CA: "from a relativistic viewpoint there is no intrinsic distinction between storage and transmission of signals. Therefore, we shall seek a single storage–transmission primitive capable of indifferently supporting either function".[16]

For instance, let us consider a signal s that connects two space-time loci, L_1 and L_2. If L_1 and L_2 are spatially separated, we will say that s was transmitted from the one to the other in a given time interval. On the other hand, if L_1 and L_2 are colocated, we will say that s was stored in that (unique) locus $L_1 \equiv L$ during a given time interval: for example,[17] s can be a message I sent to my secretary in form of e-mail (transmission) or s can be a message left on my desk in the form of note for the secretary to pick it up the following day (storage). "Thus, it is clear that the terms 'storage' and 'transmission' describe from the viewpoint of differ-

---

16 Fredkin and Toffoli [1982], p. 224; see also Margolus [1984].
17 See Fredkin and Toffoli [1982], p. 226.

ent reference frames are one and the same physical process."[18]

Now, in our universe *each single hexagonal cell performs the double function of signal storage and transmission, as it implements our MoR ϕ.* In fact we know that, when the number of active bits perceived by the cell in input is odd (and in particolar, when such number is equal to one), the single cell, by applying *Perm,* translates the signal to the next cell with "uniform rectilinear motion". Each cell thus operates as a *circuit-unit*: the role of a circuit-unit is that of moving the bit of information from one point in the grid to the adjacent point in one unit of time interval – for instance:

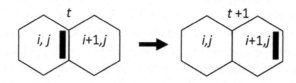

As is clear, it is possible to realize circuits of arbitrary length, taken simply as successions of circuit-units, specifically considering chains of cells that are adjacent to one another. A rectilinear circuit of length n is a path along which any signal, such as a sequence of bits, can flow, and whose extremes, given that the signal moves by exactly one cell per unit of time, are also separated by n units of time.

We notice that each cell, conceived as a circuit-unit (and thus, each rectilinear circuit realized as the juxtaposition of cells), just realizes an iterated application of *Perm*, and hence is *conservative* (it conserves in output the amount of 1s and 0s received in input in the sextuples), and it is *invertible* (because it maps distinct inputs onto distinct outputs); moreover it is *strongly* so: it coincides with its inverse, onto which it is mapped by the transformation that inverts time: $t \mapsto -t$.

Naturally, a finite memory (which is the only possible one, in accordance with the strict "finitary" requirements we specified in defining our universe) is easy to implement, by straightforwardly using sequences of bits which, through suitable "deviations" induced by means of precise collisions (we will examine some examples *infra*), move in circle; or, which form stable and periodic configurations (to be sure, in

---

[18] Ibid.

the short term: it is to be borne in mind that our universe, because of its finiteness and the reversibility of our rule, has an evolution which is made of one single, long period repeating itself if there's enough time).

But there is also a much stronger and radical sense, in which it can be stated that our universe has "memory": owing to the fact that its rule-MoR is *time-reversal invariant*, in fact, the universe retains perfect memory of its initial configuration – let us say, $\overline{\sigma}_0$ – throughout all the time of its evolution, since no bit of information is created or destroyed, and any configuration can always be retrieved due to reversibility.

The tricky part of our work consists in showing that our universe **U** is capable of processing its information on the basis of a functionally complete set of logic gates. It is well-known that in any reversible CA computation cannot but be a conditional routing of signals. Off-handedly speaking: a reversible CA must respect a criterion of *conservativity* for which "signals are treated as unalterable objects that can be moved around in the course of a computation but never created or destroyed"[19]. It is even more widely known that a boolean logic with AND, NOT and FAN-OUT or copy constitutes a universal set of logic primitives; but, as already observed, the ordinary AND is not reversibile and, intuitively, a FAN-OUT, doubling a signal, seems to imply a *creatio ex nihilo* of bits which contradicts the criterion of conservativity.

Nevertheless, these problems are solved in our universe in a surprisingly brilliant manner. The fundamental idea is as simple as it is elegant: *each single cell <i, j> of our universe can be seen as a logic gate* – or rather, specifically as a universal logic gate – just as it is a locus of transition (transmission or collision) of bits and sequences of bits of information.

First of all, we know that a conservative logic gate must have as many inputs as outputs. Now, it is easy to realize that 2-input/2-output logic gates cannot deliver the sought-after universality. In this case, in fact, we have $4^4 = 256$ possible truth-tables, and only 24 are reversible. It has been demonstrated by Margolus that all the 24 reversible tables can be reduced to compositions of the Boolean XOR, and the XOR alone is

---

[19] Fredkin and Toffoli [1982]: 227.

not universal. Therefore, we need to increase the number of input-output lines.

In the literature there are universal and reversible logic gates, such as the Fredkin gate (which has a truth table with 3 inputs and 3 outputs), but these are not easy to implement in a CA with the requirements of "physical plausibility" we are looking for.[20] We also assume number 3 as base, and we treat any single cell in our lattice as a gate taking input from three of its six sides, and generating an output from (other) three. This intuitively means that, when we want to simulate unary operators (such as NOT) or binary operators (such as AND) some inputs and outputs will be taken as "pleonastic". On the other hand, given any operator or MoR f with a certain number of inputs-outputs, it is possible to obtain an operator-MoR g "merged" in f, that is to say, having a smaller number of inputs-outputs, by assigning prespecified *constant* values (or possibly periodic, but here we do not deal with this case) to some input lines, and taking no interest in some output lines (*garbage bits*, as they are termed in the literature). Then, it can be said that the MoR f *simulates* g through constants and garbage. As we will examine later on, in Chapter 4, which is devoted to the recursion theory of MoR, the capability of merging a MoR in another one in this manner will have a certain relevance for the possibility of representing all the operators of the *traditional recursion theory* as MoR implemented in our cellular universe.

Let us consider, then, the single cell $<i, j>$; let us suppose it takes as inputs the signals arriving from the directions x, y and z (corresponding to directions 4, 5 and 6 in the conventional numeration viewed above), marked here in dark grey, and delivers as outputs the signals coming out of the three opposite sides, marked in light grey:

---

[20] The only case we know of is the *billiard ball model* by Fredkin and Toffoli [1982]; see also Toffoli and Margolus [1990].

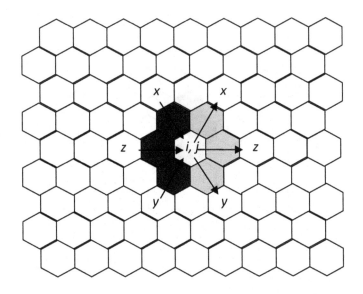

1.9.1 Conjunction

In this manner, each cell of our universe can implement a reversibile AND – that is, to express ourselves in a terminology that should be rather familiar by now: the MoR or operator **conjunction** can be seen as derived in a precise way from our fundamental rule-MoR ϕ. It is sufficient to consider z as a "control line", activated by fixing its value at $z = 1$ (that is to say, by letting come up in the direction z a sequence of "active" bits or 1s). In such a way, taking into account the bits arriving from the directions x and y, the cell produces both in the direction of exit x and in the direction of exit y an output which is the conjunction of x and y: the output of x (and of y) = 1 if and only if the input of x = 1 and that of y = 1, otherwise the output of x (and of y) = 0:

z	x	y	Output x and Output y: x AND y
1	1	1	1
1	1	0	0
1	0	1	0
1	0	0	0

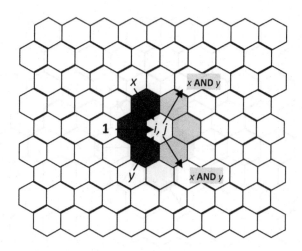

1.9.2 Negation

Each cell can also implement the negation NOT, that is, the MoR **(boolean) negation** can be derived in a precise way from our super-rule according to the same strategy: it is sufficient to fix $z = 1$ and $y = 0$. In such manner the output of z is the negation of the input of x, that is to say, if input $x = 1$, output $z = 0$, and if input $x = 0$, output $z = 1$:

z	x	y	Output z: NOT x
1	1	0	0
1	0	0	1

1.9.3 Fan-out

By having AND and NOT we already have functional completeness in view of the fact, as it is well-known, that {AND, NOT} constitutes a functionally complete set of logic operators. However we can also realize the FAN-OUT, specifically introducing a MoR, **fan-out** which duplicates signals. Obviously, in a reversible context the duplication of signals abides by precise requirements: "if we were to allow signals to split in the forward direction, we would then also have to allow two signals to 'join' in the reverse direction. We therefore require that all fan-outs occur only within individual signal processing".[21]

And this is also realized in our universe: here each individual cell can duplicate the signals, using the input pattern for negation: keeping fixed z = 1 and y = 0, any cell $<i, j>$ produces two copies of the input of x; one is directed to the same input side of z, and the other to the same input side of x.

The fact that a copy of x is redirected by the same side it came from indicates that this configuration can be also used to bounce back (*kick-back*) signals of arbitrary length.

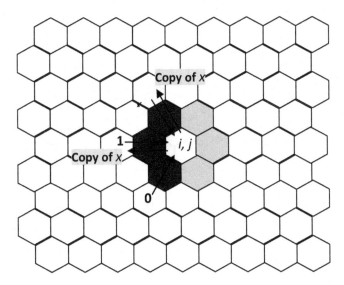

1.9.4 Delays

When constructing logic circuits it is necessary to have appropriate means to introduce deviations, kickbacks and delays. Kickback, as we know by now, is guaranteed in all cases in which an even number of "active" bits converges onto a cell, for the application of *Id*. By using the pattern for the MoR **(boolean) negation**, it is possible to set up ad hoc *translations* and *delays* of signals. The MoR **(boolean) negation** is implemented in the cells not only by reversing the incoming signals, but also by causing the negated signal to make an angle: in the example above, the signal to be negated enters in x in the cell $<i, j>$ from the direction (we conventionally labelled as) 4, and it comes out negated in direction 2. Hence, using couples of negation-cells, the second of which negates the signal negated by the first yielding back the original, it is possible to realize angles at will, for instance in circuits having this shape – where the black arrow specifies the course of a sequence of bits (for example 10110111), and the grey arrow indicates the corresponding negated sequence (for example 01001000):

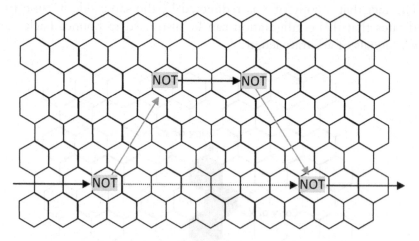

The signal thus comes out delayed by 4 units of time with respect to the dashed rectilinear trajectory.

1.10   Conclusions

We can therefore conclude that our rule-MoR, as it supports all the primitives of computation of any digital computer, is capable of universal computation; if we identify the initial configuration $\overline{\sigma_0}$ of our CA with the starting data of our universe, then its evolution is that prescribed by our rule-MoR ϕ (with the corresponding induced global rule Φ): the program with which it elaborates those data. And we know that, thanks to ϕ, this universe in its evolution can produce and host computers, that is, universal Turing machines, and thus implement any finite algorithm and evaluate any computable operator.

Furthermore, all the logical operations realizable by our cells are (1) conservative (equal number of 1s and 0s as inputs and outputs), (2) reversible, and (3) time-reversal invariant: if we reintroduce the actions of any one of these logic gates as its perceptions and we make the gate function in reverse, the result will be the original input.

Of course, for all the reversible CA (and therefore also for ours) all depends on acurately arranging the *initial configurations* of computation: in our universe, for example, it is required that the cells are "activated" at the right moment by streams of appropriate bits so that they behave as conjunctions or negations or sums, etc. However, this is inevitable when reversible rules are used: since nothing is created and nothing is destroyed from an informational standpoint, everything is to be done by moving bits appropriately. It is precisely because each bit remains in the automaton, and it is only moved from one locus to another, that the information is not dispersed in the environment and, ideally, there is no energy waste.

In the meantime, we note that, if in our universe there can exist UTMs, then it is unpredictable in a strict sense: according to the Halting Theorem, notoriously, there does not exist a general algorithm capable of predicting whether a UTM, given a certain input, will halt after n steps, thereby providing us with its output. And the same holds for the evolution of our universe, for it can implement universal computers: there does not exist a computational shortcut to predict the outcomes of its evolution. The most efficient possible emulation of the evolution of our universe is such evolution itself.

This is a critical difference between the so to speak "analytic" approach of traditional mathematics and the algorithmic-computational approach of the mathematics of the models of reference developed in this book. We cannot predict future states without running the algorithm, which means that we can anticipate the results of the algorithm only if we dispose of a way to make the algorithm run faster. But, inasmuch as the universe cannot develop at a velocity higher than the velocity at which it does develop, there are no temporal shortcuts. Since our rule-MoR is *computation-universal*, beyond a certain level of complexity of the relevant patterns, the only way to know what configurations will be produced by the universe consists in running the software that implements it starting from an initial configuration, and in standing to watch – in putting into action, in sum, an exercise of experimental mathematics. If our conjectures on the isomorphism between reality and information are correct (in particular: the logic operators can be – as a philosopher would say – "ramseyfied" through their truth table and the physical world supplies realizers for these informational roles), this will reveal itself also as an exercise of experimental *physics*.

2. Computational Formalism

In the previous chapter we showed how a single fundamental rule/MoR, implemented in each of the cells in our digital universe, realizes universal computation in a precise sense. In that chapter, we began to introduce a functional notation to represent the MoR in general, and through this we clarified what it means that a MoR is defined upon a set of possible perceptions and actions. In the present chapter we will develop the syntax of an actual *formal language*, which will be useful in the following chapters to formalize several parts of the mathematics of the models of reference through a series of axioms and definitions.

2.1 Syntax

The syntax of the formal language we will adopt is consistent with the so-called "canonical notation" of standard logic, but it entails a rather abundant symbolic equipment (and, as we will see, also the use of non-standard operators). Not all the symbols of the language will be employed in all parts of our theory: we will recognize that in order to formulate the fundamental sub-theories (our mereological account of the ontology of the MoR in the following Chapter, and the treatment of recursion in Chapter 4), a quite restrained vocabulary will suffice. On the other hand, our formalization has to allow to derive the i-ese – the universal language for the Artificial Intelligence based on MoR, in progress of development in our laboratory (cf. the related appendix to this volume). Now i-ese, besides being all-in-one with the mathematics of the MoR, will have to encompass at least the essence of the huge expressive capabilities, of natural language – that is, in substance, of ordinary languages such as Italian, English or Japanese.

The reason why we chose to make use of the canonical notation of logic is twofold:

(1) on the one hand, there are reasons of communicative convenience. Canonical notation is not termed so by chance: it is common knowledge among mathematical logicians, computer scientists, and philosophers, after prevailing over its competitors (for example, the Polish notation, Frege's bidimensional notation, etc.) Variations of this notation have been and are currently used to formalize Peano arithmetic, the theory of real numbers, set theory, the theory of recursive functions, any algebraic theory (group, field, lattice theories, etc.), order theories, theories concerning relationships of biological kinship, the theory of projective planes, etc. Furthermore, it is upon this notation that philosophical disputes over these and other subject matters are conducted. Illustrious philosophers such as Willard van Orman Quine have thus declared, after due consideration, that the canonical notation is sufficient for all scientific purposes.

(2) On the other hand, there are also more substantial reasons to use this notation, especially in the version we will present. In fact it represents a good mediation between object-oriented artificial languages, and functional application-oriented ones. The atomic formulas of the canonical notation take into account the intranscendible predicative structure of the language which, to use an expression dear to linguists, is a candidate *par excellence* for the role of "semantic universal" (we will say a few things about what semantic universals are in the aforementioned appendix). Now, in its simplest case predication consists in the sequential concatenation of an individual term with a one-place predicate ("Socrates *runs*", "Uma Thurman *is an actress*", etc.). And an individual term is precisely one used to refer to an *object*, whereas the concateneted predicate is used to refer to a property, a characteristic, or condition which is thereby ascribed to that object. The generalization to multi-place predicates is straightforward: when an n-place predicate is related to n individual terms, this is done to affirm that between the *objects* those terms refer to there subsists the relation the predicate refers to ("Socrates *eats* the apple", "Milan *is located halfway* between the pole *and* the equator", etc.). And the atomic formulas in our formal language – that is, the basic blocks starting from which more complex formulas are constructed – precisely reflect such structure: they consist (as we will show) in the concatenation of an n-place predicate letter, or predicate constant, with n individual terms which stand for the respective objects.

On the other hand, in our symbolic notation we will include, besides predicative constants, also functorial constants to directly designate operators, and the lambda operator for predicate abstraction. This means that in our language it is possible in principle to express (through rules of lambda-abstraction and lambda-reduction) "procedural" ideas of abstraction and functional application derived from the lambda calculus, which, as it is well-known, is a paradigm of functional programming languages such as the LISP or GEDANKEN. But the lambda operator can be useful to form complex predicates, that is to say, predicates provided with structure, starting from given formulas. And the possibility to construct such complex expressions, we envisage, will be essential in view of the development of i-ese. Under this aspect, our formal notation is close to languages such as the PROLOG (or better, it is these languages which are based on a logic notation such as the one we adopted), in which initial predicates are defined establishing the elements which satisfy them (*prolog facts*), and then rules (*prolog rules*) to define new predicates starting from those initially introduced are recursively specified.

2.2 Alphabet

Let us call L the formal language we are about to introduce. The alphabet of L is simply the set A of the symbols of L. The set A is subdivided into three sub-alphabets: (1) the *logical* alphabet, (2) the *descriptive* one, and (3) the *auxiliary* one.

We will now introduce the symbols of the alphabet of L presenting them in a direct way; we will subsequently provide some comments and explanations.

1. The logical vocabulary of our language will have the following symbols:

1.1. The five *logical connectives*: $\neg$, $\wedge$, $\vee$, $\rightarrow$, $\leftrightarrow$, which we will respectively call: *negation, conjunction, disjunction, conditional, biconditional*.

1.2. The two *quantifiers*: $\forall$, $\exists$, which we will respectively call *universal quantifier* and *existential quantifier*.

1.3.   Two *alethic modal operators* or *modalizers*: □ , ◊ , which we will respectively name *necessity operator* and *possibility operator*.

1.4.   Two *temporal modal operators*: F , P , which we will respectively term *future-time operator* and *past-time operator*.

1.5.   A *lambda-abstraction* operator: λ , which we will call *λ-operator*.

1.6.   A two-place predicate: = , which we will name the *identity predicate*.

2.   The descriptive alphabet of our language will have the following symbols:

2.1.   An indefinitely large number of *individual variables*, for which we will use the *italic letters*: x, y, z – and, in case we need more than three distinct variables in the same context, those same letters followed by indices, for example: x_1, x_2, … , x_n, with n a natural number.

2.2.   An indefinitely large number of *individual constants*, also called *proper nouns* or *atomic nouns*. For these we will generally employ the *italic* letters: a, b, c – and also here, in case we need more than three distinct nouns in the same context, those same letters followed by indices, for instance: c_1, c_2, … , c_n. We will nonetheless introduce specific symbols as designated individual constants, contextually providing an explanation for them.

2.3.   For each natural number $n > 0$, an indefinitely large number of *n-ary functors* or *functorial constants*, for which we will generally employ the *italic* letters: f, g, h – and also here, in case we need more than three distinct functors in the same context, those same letters followed by indices, for example: f_1, f_2, … , f_n. Occasionally it might be useful to explicitly indicate the *ariety* of a given functor, which can be done by writing it in superscript; thus for example f^2 will be a binary or two-place functor, f^3 wil be a ternary or three-place functor, …, f^n will be an *n*-ary or an *n*-place functor. At times we will use functorial constants with the role of *arbitrary nouns* for operators and MoR ("given an operator f...", etc.). We will nonetheless introduce also here specific symbols as designated functorial symbols, contextually providing an explanation for them.

2.4. For each natural number $n \geq 0$, an indefinitely large number of n-ary *predicate letters* or *predicative constants*, for which we will employ the *italic* capital letters: P, Q, R, – and also here, in case we need more than three distinct predicative constants in the same context, those same letters followed by indices, for example: P_1, P_2, ... , P_n. Occasionally, it may also be useful to explicitly indicate the *ariety* of a given predicate constant by writing it in superscript: P^2 will be a binary or two-place predicate constant, P^3 will be a ternary or three-place predicate constant, ..., P^n will be an n-ary or an n-place predicate constant. Also in this case we will introduce specific symbols as designated predicative constants, contextually providing an intuitive explanation for them. Other slight modifications to our notation may contextually be introduced, and they will always be immediately understandable.

3. The auxiliary alphabet of our language will have the following symbols:

3.1. The two round brackets, (and).

3.2. The two square brackets, [and].

3.3. The period, .

3.4. The comma, , .

As far as the constant descriptive symbols of L are concerned, it is necessary to pay attention to the following point. When presenting a formal language of the type of L, one allows oneself to introduce as many symbols as one desires for individual, predicate and functorial constants, perhaps even contextually: in sum, one can be "lavish" with the descriptive vocabulary.

On the contrary, when a particular formal system is constructed, usually a strict terminological regimen is adopted: only those explicitly mentioned in the alphabet of the theory are employed as non-logical constants. The theory itself is conceived as a formal characterization of the specific expressions in question. For instance: by using our language L it is possible to formalize elementary arithmetic with Peano's principles – as we will see in Chapter 4; in order to do so, a designated functor – let us say "*s*" – is introduced and it is explained what its intuitive interpretation is – let us assume it is established that it means "the immediate successor of"; then, the axioms, the theorems and the definitions of the formalized theory in which that functor appears, can be taken as characterizations of the meaning itself and the functioning of such functor. And when in the next Chapter we will construct a formal-axiomatic mereology using the language L with the intent of providing the details of the ontology of the MoR, we will introduce a designated predicate P; we will explain what its intuitive interpretation is, namely that it means "is part of"; and the definitions and the mereological axioms will be characterizations of the meaning of that predicate, provided within the theory.

2.3 Formation rules

An ordered *n*-tuple of symbols of A is a *string* of A. A string is simply a finite sequence of symbols which is generated by *concatenating them* (that is, for example, by writing them in a row one after the other). We will now present a sequence of rules, called *rules of formation or rules of well-formedness* for the language L on the alphabet A. The rules provide us with the "grammar" of our formal language L: they tell us which strings of A, that is to say, which finite sequences of symbols belonging to A, are well-formed expressions, that is, acceptable or grammatical, and which are not.

The rules constitute a recursive, or inductive, definition:

(B) in the *base step* of the definition, we specify the basic expressions of our language;

(P) in the *recursive step* of the definition, a series of recursive clauses tells us how to construct complex expressions from given expressions;

(C) finally, the *closure clause* or closure condition states that no string of symbols of A is a well-formed expression, except for those recursively specified by (B) and (P).

The two types of complex expressions that will be recursively defined are *individual terms* and *formulas* (at times we speak of "well-formed formulas" to distinguish them from non-well-formed formulas, specifically from strings of symbols of A which do not conform to the rules of formation; but we will normally simply talk of "formulas", intending to refer to the well-formed ones).

For our purposes it will result useful, besides having a fully formalized object language, to also occasionally employ (especially in this chapter) some *meta-symbols*, or *metalinguistic symbols*, that is, symbols that can stand for symbols of the formalized object language. This means that we will enrich the metalanguage (ordinary English) we are using to expose the language and the formal theory with a symbolic notation, in order to facilitate the reading and to make our exposition more rigorous.

In particolar, in the interest of providing the rules of formation for L we will need two types of metalinguistic variables which stand respectively (a) for *individual terms*, and (b) for *formulas* of the object-language L:

(a) we will adopt as metavariables for terms the *italic* letters: t, s, r (and also here, if needed, indices: t_1, t_2, ... , t_n);

(b) we will adopt as metavariables for formulas the *Greek* letters: α, β, γ (and also here, if needed, indices: α_1, α_2, ... , α_n).

Here follows the recursive definition of the grammatically well-formed expressions of our language.

2.3.1 Individual terms

The recursive definition of *individual term* is the following:

(B)
1.   An individual variable is an individual term.
2.   An individual constant is an individual term.

(P)

1. If f is an n-place functor, and $t_1, \ldots, t_n$ are individual terms, then $f(t_1, \ldots, t_n)$ is an individual term.[22]

(C) Nothing else, except what is specified in (B) and (P), is an individual term.

It is to be noted that, on the basis of such definition, the metavariables for terms $t_1, \ldots, t_n$ are not individual terms *of* our language L: being "meta-symbols", they function as mere placeholders: they stand to indicate that they could be replaced by full-blown terms.

Furthermore, it is to be observed that we will employ the letters $x, y, \ldots$ in an *ambiguous* manner, now as full-fledged terms (i.e., individual variables) *of* our language L, now as metavariables *for variables* of such language (hence, specifically *not* for individual *constants*).This systematically ambiguous use of such letters (now as symbols, now as meta-symbols) is in use in various standard texts of logic, it being intended that the context will always clarify by itself which type of symbols are at issue, thereby avoiding any possibility of misunderstanding.

2.3.2 Formulas

With regard to the well-formed formulas of our language L, we introduce first of all the notion of *atomic formula* via the following definition:

If $t_1, \ldots, t_n$ are individual terms, and P is any n-ary predicate constant, then an expression of the form:

$$P(t_1, \ldots, t_n)$$

is an atomic formula.

---

[22] Occasionally we will employ a different notation for particolar operators. For example, introducing a functor "+" for the addition operator, instead of writing $+(\,t_1\,,\,t_2)$ we will write the operator between the operands, in order to follow the most classic mathematical notation: $t_1 + t_2$. These and other modifications to the notation should always result readily understandable.

Hence, an atomic formula is simply a string of symbols which is made of an *n*-ary predicate letter, followed by as many terms as it is needed to saturate its *n* places (enclosed in brackets and spaced by commas). [23]

The recursive definition of the (well-formed) *formulas* of L must in fact also include a definition of *predicate*, because our λ-operator allows us to define structured predicates starting from formulas, while formulas in turn include predicates. It is therefore necessary to unitarily define it all, with a joint recursion:

(B)
1.   An atomic formula is a formula.
2.   A predicate constant is a predicate.

(P)
1.   If α is a formula, then $\neg\alpha$ is a formula;
2.   If α and β are formulas, then $(\alpha \wedge \beta)$ is a formula;
3.   If α and β are formulas, then $(\alpha \vee \beta)$ is a formula;
4.   If α and β are formulas, then $(\alpha \rightarrow \beta)$ is a formula;
5.   If α and β are formulas, then $(\alpha \leftrightarrow \beta)$ is a formula;
6.   If α is a formula, then $\square\alpha$ is a formula;
7.   If α is a formula, then $\lozenge\alpha$ is a formula;
8.   If α is a formula, then $F\alpha$ is a formula;
9.   If α is a formula, then $P\alpha$ is a formula;
10.   If α is a formula, and x an individual variable, then $\forall x\alpha$ is a formula;
11.   If α is a formula, and x an individual variable, then $\exists x\alpha$ is a formula;
12.   If α is a formula, and x an individual variable, then $[\lambda x.\alpha]$ is a predicate.
13.   If $[\lambda x.\alpha]$ is a predicate and t an individual term, then $[\lambda x.\alpha](t)$ is a formula.

(C) Nothing else, except for what is specified in (B) and (P), is a formula or a predicate.

---

[23] On the basis of the definition, an atomic formula which starts with the predicate of identity would have the form: $=(t, s)$. However, we will use the more intuitive form: $t = s$.

It is to be noted that on the basis of the definition also the Greek letters strictly speking are not formulas of the language L, given that they are not atomic formulas, nor a compound formed starting from atomic formulas; they are, instead, placeholders for which any formula can be substituted.

2.3.3 Details on the syntax

We take for granted the usual notions of symbol *occurrence*, of *scope* and *subordination* for a logic symbol (connectives and quantifiers), of *free* and *bound* for variables. A formula which contains at least one variable with a free occurrence is said to be open. Subsequently, we will denote by "$\alpha[x]$" any formula α in which the variable x is free (in at least one occurrence). A formula which does not contain any free occurrences of variables, but rather, either is devoid of variables or it contains only bound variables (in every occurrence) by quantifiers, is termed to be a *closed formula* or *sentence*. A term devoid of variables is said to be a *closed term* or a *noun*, whereas a term with variables is called an *open term*, and sometimes a *nominal form*.

An important syntactic operation on formulas is that of *substitution*. In general, given any formula α, any variable x and term t, we *define substitution of x with t in α* the formula obtained by uniformly replacing all the free occurrencies of the variable x in α with t; such formula will be designated by "$\alpha[x/t]$" – while at times we will indicate by "$\alpha[x/y]$" the fact that the variable x is in particular replaced by a different variable y (obviously, we are not excluding the "trivial" case of the substitution of a free variable with itself: if $t = x$, $\alpha[x/t]$ is just α).

We assume that the substitution $\alpha[x/t]$ is *legitimate* only if the term t is *free for x* in α, that is, only if each free occurrence of x in the formula is such that no sub-formula of α containing it starts with a quantifier or with the λ-operator which binds one of the variables occurring in the term t (or which the term t consists in). It is always assumed that the substitutions operated are legitimate. Moreover, we will adopt the usual conventions to eliminate brackets, in order to ease the reading of formulas.

In practice, we are going to piecemeal introduce the letters we need, indicating what type of symbols we are dealing with (proper nouns or *n*-ary predicative constants, *n*-ary functors, etc.) and specifying if needed their intended interpretation in the context. Possible slight modifications with respect to the standard characterization of the language should always be readily understandable, and in any case, as we were saying, they will be accompanied by contextual explanations.

Treating *n*-ary predicative constants, we did not exclude that $n = 0$. In fact, we can consider regular sentential variables of Boolean languages as a particular type (a limit-case) of atomic formulas of the language L: specifically, as that type of atomic formula in which the predicate letter is 0-ary, it is not followed by any term. Now, (a) all the base symbols of standard boolean languages are also symbols of our language L, precisely because the letters $P, Q, R, \dots$, are intended as atomic formulas, and the logic (the five connectives) and auxiliary (the brackets) symbols of boolean language also belong to the symbolic apparatus of L; furthermore, (b) the rules of formation of L permit to construct all the formulas of the normal boolean languages. Hence, each formula of a standard boolean language will also be a formula of L.

2.4 Computability of the syntax

The definition of the syntax of L is purely recursive. We might claim that the only operator at stake here is an operator or MoR (we could call it **concatenation-L**), which takes as input symbols of A, and gives as output their concatenation – for instance: it writes them one after the other. The clauses for recursion presented *supra* govern the admitted concatenations, namely they specify in an exact manner which strings, that is, concatenations of symbols of A, are admitted as grammatically well-formed in the language L.

Inasmuch as each clause of the recursion can be specified as a simple algorithmic instruction of finite size, any universal Turing machine (UTM) can implement the rules of formation, and generate and/or recognize the strings of A which are admitted as well-formed expressions of L.

In particular, a *cellular automaton* (CA) akin to the one we delineated in the previous chapter, specifically capable of universal computation, is equipped to produce/recognize any *unrestricted* formal language (that is of type *n*. 4 of the classification proposed by Noam Chomsky and referred to as *Chomsky hierarchy*).[24]

Chomsky distinguishes four types of formalized languages: (1) *regular*, (2) *context-free*, (3) *context-sensitive*, and (4) *unrestricted*. Whereas context-free grammars are used to define the syntax of most programming languages, each of these consists of strings which can be generated or recognized by automata with different capabilities of calculus and (especially) memory. Notably, one can univocally associate finite strings of symbols to individual states σ of a CA, and the states achieved after *n* units of time of computation performed by the CA to the acceptance or not, on the part of the CA, of a corresponding string as a well-formed string. Now, on the basis of our rules of formation for L we can imagine that there will be *non-terminal* strings of symbols of the alphabet, which are produced by applying single rules, but which are not yet the final string we intend to achieve. Regular languages are the most limited in non-terminal strings; the *context-free* ones allow for non-terminal strings, but there exists a fixed limit to the length of the strings that can be produced. The *context-sensitive* languages have more complex definitions, perhaps the simplest one being that context-sensitive grammars have "noncontracting" rules, that is, they do not allow strings of symbols to decrease in length. The *unrestricted* languages precisely do not have any restriction on the computable rules of the syntax. What we are interested in is that a UTM, and thus a CA capable of universal computation, can implement the syntax of a formal language of the fourth type, which is the most demanding computationally, and hence also that of the other three.[25]

The syntax of L is therefore implementable in any CA capable of universal computation. Sets of *global configurations* of a CA (that is, as we know, of instantaneous states of the set of the cells that constitute it) can be seen as formal languages; and the grammars of the languages in question can be specified by the global rules of transition, namely by the

---

[24] See Chomsky [1956]. For an overview, see Rosen [2007], Ch. 12.
[25] See Ilachinski [2001], pp. 292-4.

functions from configurations to configurations of the CA induced by the respective local rules with which the cells of the CA update their states.

2.5 The axiomatic and definitory structure

Our strategy in the following chapters will consist in treating the *axioms* we will present as "implicit definitions" of non-logical terms appearing in them, that is, equivalently to the (*explicit*) definitions we will formulate therein, as characterizations of their meaning. In particular, the role of an axiom or of a definition is to restrict the intended interpretation of our formal language L, so that certain structures are excluded. Specifically, when we say that we take a given formula of the formal language as an axiom of the theory, what we assert is that it directly characterizes reality: an axiom is a formula of our language which must be valid in every acceptable model for the interpretation of the language itself, once the domain of variation of the variables of L has been fixed.

Speaking of definitions, we can immediately present a simple and standard one, which nevertheless has great relevance for the rest of our work. Actually, it is not a single definition but rather a scheme of extremely general applicability. Our language L is endowed both with predicative terms or predicative constants and with functorial terms. The intuitive idea would be that predicate terms stand for *properties* or *relations*, and functors for *operations-functions*. However, there exists a simple and very well-known inter-definability between operations-functions and properties-relations. In fact, it is possible to associate to each n-ary relation R defined on a domain of objects, let us call it D^n, its characteristic operator, hence, MoR – we say, $c_R \colon D^n \to \{1, 0\}$ such that:

$$c_R(x_1, \ldots, x_n) = \begin{cases} 1 & \text{if } <x_1, \ldots, x_n> \in R \\ 0 & \text{otherwise} \end{cases}$$

Vice versa, it is always possible to associate to any operator f with n inputs the respective $n+1$-ary relation G_f (mathematicians speak of its *graph*), which exactly subsists between the inputs of f and the corresponding outputs, that is, the relation such that:

$<x_1, \ldots, x_n> \in G_f$ if and only if $f(x_1, \ldots, x_n) = x_n+1$.

Therefore, in general discourses phrased in terms of properties and relations are always reducible to discourses in terms of operators, and vice versa. From the standpoint of syntax, this means that we can always define *functors* of L through appropriate *predicates* of L (which satisfy certain conditions of existence and unicity), and vice versa. We will make an extensive use of this inter-definability in Chapter 4, devoted to the recursive MoR.

2.6 Inference rules

If the basic assertions of our formal system are constituted by its axioms, we need an "inferential device" to safely derive the theorems from the axioms. Since all derivations will be attainable by using classical elementary logic, the single proofs are totally canonical and it is not necessary to report them; however, we will present a couple of examples of explicit deductions of theorems from axioms in the next Chapter. Deductions will be linearly constructed and we will use the classical Gentzen calculus of natural deduction. A (typical) natural deduction system has the advantage of being devoid of logical axioms, and of having only logical inference rules. Hence, it reflects in the syntax an important conceptual difference: whereas axioms and definitions will be the principles regulating the descriptive symbols of the language, specify-ing, as we were mentioning, constraints for the models of the theory, logical inference rules will be employed to logically derive the theorems from those principles. On the other hand, different settings for the logic apparatus – for instance, Hilbert-Frege style axiomatic calculus, or se-quent calculus – would be equivalent, inasmuch as these versions of classical elementary calculus are demonstrably sound and complete, that is to say they allow to derive all and only the logical consequences of the axioms.

In natural deduction there is a rule called introduction rule, and one named elimination rule, for each of the logical connectives and quantifier symbols (except for the case of negation, which is classically slightly more complex). In general, given a logical symbol $, an elimination rule for $ (marked as "E$") contains it as its main operator in the premise, or in one of the premises, and it tells us what we can infer from it. An introduction rule for $ (marked as "I$"), instead, tells us how to derive a conclusion that contains $ as its main operator from certain premises. A specific *assumption* rule is then used to introduce the required axioms or hypotheses into the demonstration.

The rules for the sentential operators are the following (where "[α]"expresses that assumption α is discarded):

$$\frac{\alpha \to \beta,\ \alpha}{\beta}\ (E\to)$$

$$[\alpha]$$
$$\vdots$$
$$\frac{\beta}{\alpha \to \beta}\ (I\to)$$

$$\frac{\alpha \land \beta}{\alpha} \quad \frac{\alpha \land \beta}{\beta}\ (E\land)$$

$$\frac{\alpha,\ \beta}{\alpha \land \beta}\ (I\land)$$

$$[\alpha]\quad [\beta]$$
$$\vdots \quad \vdots$$
$$\frac{\alpha \lor \beta,\ \gamma,\ \gamma}{\gamma}\ (E\lor)$$

$$\frac{\alpha}{\alpha \lor \beta} \quad \frac{\beta}{\alpha \lor \beta}\ (I\lor)$$

$$\frac{\alpha,\ \neg\alpha}{\beta}\ (E\neg)$$

$$\frac{\neg\neg\alpha}{\alpha}\ (DN)$$

$$[\alpha] \quad [\alpha]$$

$$\vdots \quad \vdots$$

$$\frac{\beta \, , \ \neg\beta}{\neg\alpha} \ (I\neg)$$

In the case of negation, the third rule (DN) serves to recapture the classical calculus and to have indirect or non-constructive proofs. The rules for the quantifiers and identity are the following:

$$\frac{\forall x \alpha}{\alpha[x/t]} \ (E\forall) \qquad\qquad \frac{\alpha[x]}{\forall y \alpha[x/y]} \ (I\forall)$$

$$[\alpha[x]] \qquad\qquad\qquad \frac{\alpha[x/t]}{\exists x \alpha} \ (I\exists)$$

$$\vdots$$

$$\frac{\exists y \alpha[x/y] \, , \ \gamma}{\gamma} \ (E\exists)$$

$$\frac{t = s \, , \ \alpha[x/t]}{\alpha[x/s]} \quad \frac{t = s \, , \ \alpha[x/s]}{\alpha[x/t]} \ (E=) \qquad\qquad \frac{}{t = t} \ (I=)$$

The rule (I∀) has the following restrictions: (a) y must not occur free in α, (b) the rule can be applied only if α[x] does not depend on assumptions in which the same variable x occurred free. (E) has the following restrictions: (a) y must not occur free in α, (b) x must not occur free in any of the assumptions used to derive the conclusion γ from α[x] (c) finally, x must not be free even in γ, that is, in the conclusion we want to derive.

Now that we are equipped with all the syntactical apparatus we need, we can start from the next Chapter with the formalization of our theory.

3. The Ontology of the Models of Reference

In the Introduction to this book we explained in an informal manner how the computational universe inhabited by our atom-cells is structured, and that in our opinion it represents a valid working hypothesis for maximizing the isomorphism between matter and information, which constitutes the basis of our approach. Now the time has come to make formally precise those descriptions: in the present chapter we develop the *ontology* of the MoR through the simple logical formalism introduced in the previous chapter.

We will employ a classical and very intuitive *mereological* framework. A *mereology* is simply a theory that characterizes the notion, hence the MoR, **parthood**, and which can be axiomatized by using our formal language L. As we already hinted at, we consider the axioms as implicit definitions of the non-logical terms that appear therein (besides, obviously, using also explicit definitions), which restrict the intended interpretation: an axiom must be true in every acceptable model, once the relevant domain of objects has been specified. In particular, the axioms of our mereological theory are formulated starting with a designated two-place predicate of our formal language L, the predicate "*P*", whose intuitive interpretation is exactly that according to which it expresses the operator **parthood**. By means of this we will be able to formally define other fundamental notions of our theory, which have previously been characterized only intuitively –such notions as those of **atom, system, internal** and **external**.

3.1 Lexical axioms

The order in which the axioms will be introduced is not random: in fact we proceed from *weaker* axioms to *stronger* principles. "Weak" and "strong", in this context, are to be intended as follows: an axiom is weak when it fixes the merely lexical meaning of the predicate *P*. A weak axiom is relatively non-controversial: it must hold for the predicate *P*, if

P is to express the notion of parthood, rather than something else. A stronger axiom, instead, is more controversial: its selection (and therefore the rejection of the models that do not satisfy it) reflects a precise *theoretic option* which must be justified. As we will see, the choice of the stronger axioms of our theory is congruent with our base ideas: our discretism, our conventionalism, and our convinction that reality, conceived in terms of MoR, is "hyper-extensional" in a specific sense.

Finally, it is to be noted that the quantification incorporated in our mereological axioms is to be intended as *absolutely unrestricted*. This means that the axioms, the relation of parthood they formalize, and the notions defined, such as those of internal, external, etc., hold for *any* type of entity. Our mereology thus presents itself as a widely general formal theory, at the same level of formal logic.[26]

Three axioms fix the fundamental meaning of **parthood**:

(A1) $\forall x P(x, x)$.
(A2) $\forall x \forall y (P(x, y) \land P(y, x) \to x = y)$.
(A3) $\forall x \forall y \forall z (P(x, y) \land P(y, z) \to P(x, z))$.

From an algebraic point of view, (A1)-(A3) tell us that the notion expressed by P is a partial order – a reflexive (A1), antisymmetric (A2) and transitive (A3) relation. That they fix the essential meaning of the expression "is a part of" is clear: (A1) guarantees that each object is a part of itself. (A2) ensures that two distinct objects cannot be part of each other. (A3) makes sure that any part of a part of an object is itself a part of that object.

Through predicate P of the language L, taken as primitive, we can define several fundamental predicates of mereological theory. If we abide by the fundamental symmetry between syntax and semantics we assumed in the previous chapter (and which will become clearer in the appendix on the *i-ese*), to these predicates there will correspond operators, and thus, MoR. We can consider the MoR defined through the MoR **parthood** as derived with respect to it, and therefore take **parthood** as primitive with respect to them.

---

[26] For the axiomatization that follows we have mostly rested upon Casati and Varzi [1999], Varzi [2003]. The classic text on the notion of parthood is Simons [1987].

Firstly, we can easily define the MoR **proper parthood**, which will be designated by the predicate PP of the language L:

(Df PP) $PP(x, y) =_{df} P(x, y) \wedge \neg P(y, x).$

The formal definition tells us that any object x is a proper part of the object y if and only if x a part of y, but y is not a part of x. From the axioms (A1)-(A3) and from (Df PP) there follow three theorems:

(T1) $\forall x \neg PP(x, x).$

(T2) $\forall x \forall y (PP(x, y) \rightarrow \neg PP(y, x)).$

(T3) $\forall x \forall y \forall z (PP(x, y) \wedge PP(y, z) \rightarrow PP(x, z)).$

As an example, here is the natural deduction formal proof of (T1):

(1)	1	$PP(x, x)$	Ass
(2)	1	$P(x, x) \wedge \neg P(x, x)$	1, DfPP
(3)		$\neg PP(x, x)$	1, 2, E¬
(4)		$\forall x \neg PP(x, x)$	3, I∀

And here is the formal proof of (T2):

(1)	1	$PP(x, y)$	Ass
(2)	1	$P(x, y) \wedge \neg P(y, x)$	1, DfPP
(3)	1	$\neg P(y, x)$	2, E∧
(4)	4	$P(y, x) \wedge \neg P(x, y)$	Ass
(5)	4	$P(y, x)$	4, E∧
(6)	1, 4	$P(y, x) \wedge \neg P(y, x)$	3, 5, I∧
(7)	1	$\neg (P(y, x) \wedge \neg P(x, y))$	4, 6, I¬
(8)	1	$\neg PP(y, x)$	7, DfPP
(9)		$PP(x, y) \rightarrow \neg PP(y, x)$	1, 8, I→
(10)		$\forall y (PP(x, y) \rightarrow \neg PP(y, x))$	9, I∀
(11)		$\forall x \forall y (PP(x, y) \rightarrow \neg PP(y, x))$	10, I∀

From an algebraic standpoint, the notion **proper parthood** is transitive (T3), asymmetric (T2) and irreflexive (T1), hence, a strict partial order. (T1) guarantees that no object is a proper part of itself; (T2), that if an object is a proper part of another, the latter is not a proper part of the former; (T3), that any proper part of a proper part of an object is itself a proper part of that object.

It is to be noted that in this system the MoR **parthood** is primitive with respect to the MoR **proper parthood**, since the latter is defined by means of the former. However, this is not the only possible account – and here is another aspect in which our conventionalist perspective emerges. From the initial axioms and from (Df PP), in fact there follows the theorem:

(T4) $\forall x \forall y (P(x, y) \leftrightarrow PP(x, y) \lor x = y)$,

That is to say, an object is a part of another if and only if, either it is a proper part of the other, or it is identical to it (this is just the ordinary connection between a non-strict partial order and the corresponding strict one). In the notion of parthood, inasmuch as it is governed by the axioms (A1) and (A2), identity is in fact taken as a limit or "improper" case of the parthood relation (in particular, (A2) tells us that the identity between x and y is implied by the fact that each is a part of the other). We might always proceed in reverse, taking PP as a primitive mereological notion, regulated by (T1)-(T3) which this time would figure as the basis axioms of the theory, and then defining **parthood**, P, as a derived notion:

(Df P) $P(x, y) =_{df} PP(x, y) \lor x = y$.

As usual, all depends on unambiguously distinguishing the initial notions, and on being clear about one's intended direction. It is conceptually a very important fact that in our theory identity can be considered as limit case of the parthood relation: this means that the notion of identity is reducible to the MoR **parthood**, taken as a mereological primitive. On the basis of axiom (A2), in fact, it is possible to have the following definition:

(Df =) $x = y =_{df} P(x, y) \land P(y, x)$

If we accept this definition, then stating that one thing is identical to another simply means: "the former is a part of the latter and the latter is a part of the former". Identity then becomes *eliminable* from our theory: we could replace the axiom (A2) with the following axiom schema (which could be called "Leibniz's mereological law"):

(A2b) $\forall x \forall y (P(x, y) \wedge P(y, x) \rightarrow (\alpha[x] \rightarrow \alpha[y]))$.

That is: if x and y are part of one another, then they are indiscernible.

Other interesting MoR can be introduced as derived, defining them through the MoR **parthood. Overlap** is one of them. Let us assume that this is expressed by the predicate K. Then we will have:

(Df K) $K(x, y) =_{df} \exists z (P(z, x) \wedge P(z, y))$.

To say that an object overlaps another is equivalent to simply stating that there is something which is a part of both – for instance, in the figure below x consists of seven light grey, flower-shaped hexagons – we term this object Grey; y consists of seven black hexagons having the same configuration – we name this object Black; and z (their overlap) consists in the two dark grey hexagons which are part of both x and y:

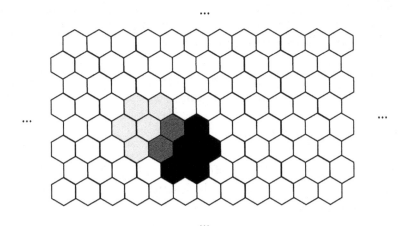

The notion of overlap is demonstrably reflexive and symmetric (but not transitive):

(T5) $\forall x K(x, x)$.
(T6) $\forall xy (K(x, y) \rightarrow K(y, x))$.

These two theorems thus guarantee two rather obvious facts: everything overlaps itself (T5), and if one thing overlaps another, then also the latter overlaps the former (T6).

Another interesting MoR is **underlap**, the dual of **overlap**. Let us assume that this is expressed by the predicate U, and we will have:

(Df U) $U(x, y) =_{df} \exists z(P(z, x) \wedge P(z, x))$

3.2 Atom-cells

Let us now come to less obvious facts. As recalled several times already, one of the basic assumptions of our research regarding the reality that surrounds us is that it is *discrete* (and, specifically, ultimately composed of simple cells that must be the minimum space-time units), and *finitistically* describable, so that for us the notion of infinity in act is merely ideal, not real. This, as we were saying, is the intended model of our theorization. From a mereological standpoint, this means that it is necessary to add an axiom to our theory, which excludes from the set of acceptable models all those in which the divisibility of reality into parts proceeds to infinity. Any theory that rejects this point, in fact, can only have models of infinite cardinality.

We start by introducing into our language an atomic predicate, A, through the following formal definition:

(Df A) $A(x) =_{df} \neg \exists y PP(y, x)$.

The definition ensures that "atom" means "object which does not have any proper parts". The atoms in our intended model are, precisely, all and only our cells.

Now, we formulate the following fourth axiom of our formal theory:

(A4) $\forall x \exists y (A(y) \wedge P(y, x))$

The axiom guarantees that any object has atoms as its ultimate parts, that is to say (in our intended interpretation), cells: there are no *atomless gunks*, portions of reality which are decomposable to infinity.

3.3 Hyper-extensionality

The fifth axiom of our theory is called "principle of strong supplementation" in the literature:

(A5) $\forall x \forall y (\neg P(x, y) \rightarrow \exists z (P(z, x) \wedge \neg K(z, y)))$.

This axiom ensures that if one object is not part of another, then there is a third object which constitutes the remainder, namely, which is a part of the former but does not overlap with the latter.

Also (A5) is a strong axiom, that is, it does not follow from the lexical meaning of "parthood". In fact, accepting (A5) means excluding from the admissible models those in which distinct objects are composed of the same proper parts. As a consequence of this, our mereology is not only extensional, as set theory is, but rather *hyperextensional*.

Set theory rules out the possibility that there are different sets with precisely the same members, as per the Principle of Extensionality.[27] However, it does admit that we can have different objects constructed from the same basis set: given an object *o*, we have $\{o\}$, $\{\{o\}\}$, $\{\{\{o\}\}\}$,…, (that is, the singleton of that object, the singleton of the singleton, etc.), and they are all distinct. On the contrary, a mereology including (A5) is "more than extensional" because it is consistent with the famous maxim by Nelson Goodman: "no distinction of entities without a distinction of content".[28]

The fact that our mereology admits a finite limit (provided by the cells) to the decomposition into parts allows a simplification of the axiomatic formulation. In principle, it would be possible to replace (A4) and (A5) with a single axiom formulated as follows:

(A4b) $\forall x \forall y (\neg P(x, y) \rightarrow \exists z (A(z) \wedge P(z, x) \wedge P(z, y)))$.

---

[27] Formulable as: $\forall x (x \in y \leftrightarrow x \in z) \rightarrow y = z$.

[28] See Goodman [1956], p. 26.

On the basis of the conventionalism that animates our perspective, we can choose the formulation we prefer (and generally: when it turns out that some axioms are reducible to others, that is to say, they are not independent but can be derived from these others as theorems, it will be sufficient to move them from the "box" of primitive axioms to that of derived principles: once it has been clarified what notions are preferred to be assumed as primitive, all the rest will fall into place).

The fundamentally hyperextensional nature of reality is then expressed by the following theorem, derivable from (A4b):

$$\text{(T7)} \quad \forall x \forall y \forall z (A(z) \rightarrow (P(z, x) \leftrightarrow P(z, y))) \rightarrow x = y).$$

This axiom rules out that there be distinct objects composed of exactly the same atoms, that is, the same elementary cells. In particular, it implies that there are no complex objects, namely aggregates of atom-cells, which are distinct but with the same proper parts. In all the cases in which we deem we have to distinguish between objects that have the same proper parts, such difference thus is not to be taken at the level of reality: we can see a thing as a cat; or as the aggregate of cells of that cat; or as the mass of molecules that compose it; or as a complex system constituted of a huge number of elementary cells; all these are however different *levels of description* of one and the same reality.

3.4 Individuability, sequentiality and istantaneity

The principle of hyper-extensionality is controversial especially if we consider entities that exist at different times, that is, if we have *cross-temporal objects*. If the variables in (T7) vary on objects that exist at different instants of time, or in different situations, the principle seems to be too strong to provide a reduction of the notion of identity. However, things change if (T7) refers to *synchronic* identity in the *current* circumstance.[29] We therefore assume that reality is *four-dimensional*, or, more exactly, *sequential*: objects can have spatial and temporal parts, so that the predicate P must be relativized to space and time. Then, garden-ordinary objects are taken as sequences of (aggregates of) instantaneous objects.

---

[29] As noted in Varzi [2003], § 3.2.

Let us develop the idea.

Assuming the idea of absolute space and time, we can exactly specify each of the atom-cells as an ordered n-tuple of space-time points. In turn, the spatial placement of an atom-cell (in the 3D case) is an ordered triple of coordinates – let us say, $<i, j, k>$ – so that on the whole, for each cell c, $c = <<i, j, k>, t>$. Each atom in our universe is thus fully distinguishable and numerically expressible.

However, the domain of the objects of the model of our theory is not only made of atom-cells, but also of aggregates of cells. The mereological axioms are constraints on the model (or better, on the structure of any admissible model), precisely because they determine what objects exist starting from the cells. Now we can wholly characterize the notion of sequentiality as follows. Assuming that reality is sequential equals assuming that, given two cells $c_1 = <<i_1, j_1, k_1>, t_n>$, $c_2 = <<i_1, j_1, k_1>, t_{n+1}>$, where t_{n+1} is the instant of time immediately subsequent to t_n, c_1 and c_2 are always *distinct*. Intuitively, c_1 and c_2 are *two* cells that occupy the same position at two consecutive instants of time, and they are distinct because there is no identity across times.

The same holds also on a macro-scale. Any system (we will formally define the notion of *system* quite soon, but it is already known at an intuitive level) finds its strict identity only at a specific time t_n because at time t_{n+1} in general, the cells involved in the description of the system will instantiate different states from those at t_n. The cat at t_n and the cat at t_{n+1} are, strictly speaking, two distinct cats. However, we treat them as "identical" because they much resemble each other. Ordinary objects are sequences of instantaneous objects. On the other hand, both for the sake of simplicity in the exposition, and to adhere to the everyday language, we can speak as if the same objects existed at different times; this holds also for the cells that, in our intended model, constitute the minimum space-time units – just as, however, we have done from the beginning of our exposition. We can say that "the same cell has passed (let us assume) from the state σ_1 to the state σ_2, on the basis of the rules $\rho_1, ..., \rho_n$". This is a sloppy way to claim: a cell c_1 in the state σ_1 at the instant of time t_n is followed, on the basis of the rules $\rho_1, ..., \rho_n$, by a cell c_2 in the state σ_2 at t_{n+1}, and c_1 and c_2 have the same spatial coordinates i_1, j_1, k_1.

3.5 Conventionalism

3.5.1 Unrestricted mereological composition

We now introduce two other very important MoR: **fusion** and **mereological product**. Let them be respectively expressed by two functors of our language L, say $\oplus$ and $\otimes$. These are defined as follows:

$$(\text{Df }\oplus)\ x \oplus y =_{df} \iota z \forall x_1 (S(x_1, z) \leftrightarrow (K(x_1, x) \vee K(x_1, y)))$$

$$(\text{Df }\otimes)\ x \otimes y =_{df} \iota z \forall x_1 (P(x_1, z) \leftrightarrow (P(x_1, x) \wedge P(x_1, y)))^{30}$$

The first definition tells us that the fusion of two objects is that unique object that has as parts precisely the parts of the two objects in question: the fusion of two objects is therefore the smallest thing the two objects are part of. If we again take as x and y, respectively, Grey and Black, that is, the two partially overlapping small aggregates of seven hexagons we have seen above, then their mereological fusion (let us term it as GreyBlack) is the object composed of all and only the non-white cells of the drawing:

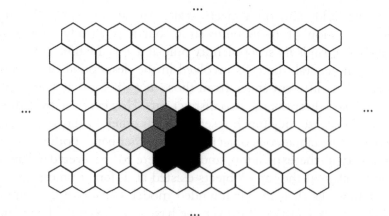

The second definition tells us that the mereological product of two objects is the unique object that has as parts precisely the parts shared by the two objects in question: the mereological product of two objects is

---

30 On the basis of the syntax of L described in the previous chapter, we should write "$x \oplus y$" but we will employ the notation "$x \otimes y$". The symbol "ι" is a descriptor, whose intuitive translation is "the only... such that...".

therefore the largest object which is part of both. In the case exemplified in the illustration, the mereological product of Grey and Black – let us call it DarkGrey – is the object composed by the two dark grey cells, which are common to Grey and Black.

We can now formulate another important axiom of our theory:

(A6) $\forall x \forall y (K(x, y) \to \exists z (z = x \otimes y))$.

This guarantees that if any two objects overlap, then there exists their mereological product.

Does a principle dual of (A6) regarding fusion exist? The answer is affirmative, and in the mereology adopted such dual principle is correspondingly stronger than (A6) for it doesn't need to be expressed in conditional form like (A6). In order to understand why, let us begin by introducing this seventh axiom:

(A7) $\exists x \forall y (P(y, x))$.

This guarantees the existence of a "total object", namely, one of which anything is part. On account of the hyper-extensionality of our theory, this object – let it be u – will be unique, and thus we can define it by means of a descriptor:

(Dfu) $u =_{df} \iota x \forall y P(y, x)$

As a consequence, the dual axiom of (A6) does not need to be in conditional form and can be formulated as follows:

(A8) $\forall x \forall y \exists z (z = x \oplus y)$

This principle in the literature is called "unrestricted mereological composition": it guarantees that, given *any* two things, there will *always* exist their fusion.

Axioms (A6) and (A8) give the closure properties of the intended model with respect to the operators **fusion** and **mereological product**, intended as finitary operators. On the other hand, we do not need axioms that characterize the corresponding infinitary operations, in accordance with our strict finitism. The mereology presented here, hence, differs on this point from the classical mereology of Tarski and Goodman.

Whereas there is the universal individual u, there is no null individual, that is:

(A9) $\neg \exists x \forall y P(x, y)$.

This principle excludes the existence of an object which is a part of everything.

3.5.2 Arbitrary *cookie-cutting*

This mereological framework is, again, consistent with the underlying conventionalism which animates our perspective. In fact, it prescribes that there does not exist a pre-established limit to what qualifies as an object. To begin with, the elementary cells are objects. But also any arbitrary aggregate of other objects and, therefore, of cells, is an object. And, finally, the universe, intended as the aggregate of all the elementary cells that exist, counts as an object in its turn.

The axiom (A8) commits us to the existence of a quantity of bizarre objects, such as the entity constituted of (whose parts are, we assume) the right half of David Lewis's left shoe, the Moon, and the fusion of the queen of England's ear-rings. The fact that such entities may result bizarre can be explained through the phenomenon of *contextual restriction* of quantification, that is, of the domain on which the variables bound by the quantifiers $\forall$ and $\exists$ are taken to vary. For example, when we state that all the beer is in the fridge,[31] plausibly, we are not asserting that all the beer in the world is held in the fridge. Rather, we are neglecting a substantial part of the beer in circulation. Probably, we mean something like "All the beer we have at home is in the fridge". We are therefore restricting our quantification to things that are at home. But it is not necessary to declare the restriction in an explicit manner: it can be easily inferred from the context:

---

[31] The well-known example is by David Lewis [1986], p. 3.

We are happy enough with mereological sums of things that contrast with their surroundings more than they do with one another; and that are adjacent, stick together, and act jointly [...]. We have no names for the mereological sum of the right half of my left shoe, plus the Moon plus the sum of all Her Majesty's ear-rings, except for the long and clumsy name I just gave it [...]. It is very sensible to ignore such a thing in our everyday thought and language. But ignoring it won't make it go away.[32]

We tend to focus ourselves, in the memorable words of Austin, on "moderate-sized specimens of dry goods", without paying too much attention to things that are too small, too big, or too fragmented, and we consequently tend to contextually restrict our quantification. This is however irrelevant when we consider the formal axioms that must go-vern our model of reality: from a conventionalist standpoint, any restric-tion of mereological fusion would be unjustified.

3.5.3 System, internal, external

In the informal introduction to the book we defined a *system* as any aggregate of adjacent cells in the space. If any fusion of objects is an object in its turn, thus, not any aggregate of atom-cells can count as a *system*. In order for an aggregate to count as a system, it must satisfy certain minimum topological requirements. Some mereological sums are fragmented, that is, "scattered" (as it is said in the literature on the sub-ject), so that they do not have the necessary adjacency between their parts.

If we therefore introduce a predicate S of our formal language L to express the notion of **system** within our theory (that is to say, a predi-cate such that the intuitive interpretation of the formula "$S(x)$" is: "x is a system"), we know that this will have to abide by some specific con-straints. These will again be formulable in axiomatic form, namely as constraints on the acceptable models.

First of all, we establish that in order to have a system at least two cells are required; hence we introduce the following axiom:

(A10) $\forall x(A(x) \rightarrow \neg S(x))$.

---

[32] Ibid., pp. 211-3.

This guarantees that no atom in our universe – and therefore, no cell, in the intended interpretation – is a system. We can then introduce a binary contact predicate, C, to express the idea of adjacency between any given objects. Now, a system is a particular type of mereological fusion; and we can admit an axiom of quasi-unrestricted composition for systems, which meets the adjacency requirement:

(A11) $\forall x \forall y (x \neq y \wedge C(x, y) \rightarrow \exists z (z = x \oplus y \wedge S(z)))$.

This principle ensures that the mereological fusion of at least two adjacent objects is a system. As it is that the application of the notion of object, namely of aggregate of cells, is arbitrary on account of the unrestricted composition, so it is for that of system. In a sense, also systems are "in the eye of who is watching". However, the arbitrariness of the concept of system does not prevent its use, but rather plays an essential role in our reasoning: we see the world in terms of systems that "perceive", "think", and "act". Finally, we can define in mereological terms the fact that something belongs to the *internal world* of a system. Let us introduce the predicate constant I, characterized by the following axiom:

(A12) $\forall x \forall y (S(x) \rightarrow (I(y, x) \leftrightarrow P(y, x)))$.

This axiom guarantees that the internal world of any system x is the aggregate of the objects that are a part of it. Symmetrically, to be the *external world* of a system, E, will signify:

(A13) $\forall x \forall y (S(x) \rightarrow (E(y, x) \leftrightarrow \neg P(y, x)))$.

The external world of a system is the mereological complement of its internal world: it is the aggregate of the objects that are *not* part of it.

We can therefore introduce predicates structured by means of the λ-operator of our formal language L, which are referred to specific systems. Let s be an individual constant of L which designates a given system; then $[\lambda x.I(x, s)]$ expresses the property, which an object can enjoy, of belonging to the internal world of s; whereas $[\lambda x.E(x, s)]$ indicates the complementary property of belonging to the external world of s.

Note that on the basis of (A12) and (A13), the notions of ***internal*** and *external* are relative: what counts as internal world and what as external world simply depends on what system s we are taking into consideration. Such arrangement of the notions of internal and external is extremely important to us: on the one hand, because it naturally conforms with our conventionalist view on the boundaries of the universe; on the other hand, because it allows to maximize the isomorphism between matter and information, thereby avoiding a series of typically philosophical pseudo-problems with regard to the distinction between mind and body, or between thought and reality. In traditional philosophy, mental phenomena, thoughts, and facts qualified as intentional are typically intended as "internal" (to the mind), whereas physical and material phenomena are typically intended as belonging to the "external world". But now we ascertain that in our arrangement the halo of mystery surrounding this distinction vanishes. Our perspective is hyperextensional also in this sense: internal phenomena are, uncomplicatedly and in the final analysis, computational processes and modifications of the states of the cells occurring in a certain place of the universe, and which are qualified as internal in relation to a given system, that is, an aggregate of cells. External phenomena are the same thing, but they are qualified as external with respect to a given system. The same is valid for our characterizations of input and output for the models of reference: a "perception" received in input is simply a modification of the internal world of a system caused by a modification of the external world; processes of thought or elaboration of information, and physical processes, are the same processes, seen as internal or as external in relation to a given system.

4. Recursive Models of Reference

When we claim "everything is a model of reference" we mean what we are saying. We are guided by the idea that the notion of MoR can capture the general concept of *operator* and that many other general notions can be reduced to it. And when we maintain that the mathematics of the MoR is a mathematics of thought we want to affirm, as we have been declaring since the introduction, that the theory of the MoR can provide a formal and mathematically respectable characterization of notions concerning phenomena such as cogntion and thought in general, otherwise treated in an intuitive and approximate manner.

The very notion of *concept* can be dealt with within the theory. Such a notion has been the core of many philosophical and scientific discussions for more than two thousand years, and almost all of its aspects are controversial. Concepts have sometimes been reduced to physical and material entities, other times, elevated to the status of platonic Ideas. They have been treated as mental representations, at times as faculties of the soul, sometimes as Fregean *Sinne*, etc. Now we dare say that concepts are *nothing but* MoR considered in their informational sense: a concept is a *rule* that relates to a given incoming signal, or perception, or input, a certain determinate outgoing signal, or output, or action, following an elaboration or thought. Therefore we can say that the models of reference are "concepts at work", or, more modestly: that by accepting to conventionally identify the traditional notion of concept with that of MoR, and by formally developing the latter, we are able to accomplish an insightful clarification of the former.

The fact that the MoR are deterministic operators in a discrete world allows us to import in our theory several notions that are typical of the standard theory of *mathematical operations* and *algorithmic functions*. Reformulating such notions in terms of MoR serves a twin purpose: on the one hand, we clarify the notion of MoR by making use of ideas which are familiar to anyone possessing the corresponding mathematical skills. On the other hand, those same ideas gain a new sense, as they are read through the general theory of MoR. This is what we will be dealing with in the present chapter.

4.1 Equivalent models of reference

When introducing an ontological category (and naturally, the MoR are a fundamental ontological category from the viewpoint of physical reality, besides having an informational aspect), it is recommendable to establish a criterion of identity for the entities in that category. Informally, a criterion of identity K for a a type of objects T is a criterion for determining, given any x or y of type T, whether or not x is the same object as y. In principle the criterion K must always (that is, precisely for any x or y) allow us to give an answer to such question. The philosopher and logician Willard Van Orman Quine claimed that any type T of objects or ontological category can be admitted into "the furniture of the world", that is, into the universal ontological catalogue, only if a criterion K for objects of type T is available; and he summarized this ontological constraint as the famous motto "No entity without identity".

From our conventionalist perspective we would rather speak of "criteria of equivalence" between MoR: to paraphrase Ludwig Wittgenstein, "every MoR is what it is, and not another MoR". However, MoR can be considered equivalent insofar as they fall in the appropriate equivalence classes, and conventionally identified, for specific purposes. Depending on such purposes, different criteria of equivalence, more or less strict, will result convenient.

Let "$\approx$" be a designated two-place predicate, indicating in our formal theory a generic relation of equivalence defined on the set M of the operators or MoR. Each relation of equivalence must of course be reflexive, symmetric, and transitive, that is to say, it must satisfy the following three axioms - where f, g and h are arbitrary functorial terms for MoR:

(A1) $f \approx f$
(A2) $f \approx g \rightarrow g \approx f$
(A3) $f \approx g \wedge g \approx h \rightarrow f \approx h$

Each relation of equivalence will determine a partition of the set M of

MoR into disjoint subsets or equivalence classes: each MoR in a given equivalence class will be in a relation $\approx$ (in the relation expressed by "$\approx$") to all the other MoR in that equivalence class, and it will not be in that relation to any other MoR.

Now we can express criteria of equivalence for MoR in our formal language L by introducing principles of the following form (principles whose general form is captured by the following schema):

(CE) $(\alpha[x/f] \leftrightarrow \alpha[x/g]) \rightarrow f \approx g$

Where the criterion, strictly speaking, is expressed by the antecedent of the conditional (EC) and α stands for a selected condition: any two given MoR f and g can be considered equivalent in a particular sense if they both satisfy a certain condition α. Depending on what is our focus in a given context, we can choose different conditions α and consequently have different criteria of equivalence.We will now consider some of these.

4.1.1 Conventional equivalences between MoR

We can formulate a first minimal condition on any relation of equivalence $\approx$ between MoR by stating the following: for any two MoR f and g to be minimally equivalent (we will adopt the notation "$f \approx_0 g$"), it is certainly necessary that they share the respective domains of perceptions and actions on which they are defined (if a model of reference can perceive things that another cannot perceive, the two are not equivalent for sure).

This is a necessary but not sufficient condition for $\approx_0$ to hold between f and g. Intuitively, in order for the minimal equivalence to hold, it must also be the case that the MoR "do the same things", at least in the sense that they produce the same actions given the same perceptions. For instance, the model of reference (a "wrong" one in relation to our highway code conventions) *traversing a crossing (only) on a red light* is probably defined for the same perceptions and actions as the model of reference *traversing a crossing (only) on a green light*, but naturally the former associates a totally different set of actions with a given input such as "perception of red light" with respect to the latter.

Hence, we can state the following condition:

Minimal criterion of equivalence between models of reference: given any two MoR $f: A \Rightarrow B$, and $g: C \Rightarrow D$, if:

(a) $A = C$ and $B = D$, that is the models are defined on the same sets of perceptions and actions;

(b)   For any input or perception $x_1, x_2, ..., x_n$ (in this order), f and g give the same output y;

Then, $f \approx_0 g$.

This type of equivalence is however a very weak condition as it does not include the *time* factor. A stricter equivalence, denoted by $\approx_1$, will take into consideration not only the correspondence between perceptions and actions of the two MoR, but also the time units they employ, given a specific input, to deliver the respective output. Thus, we will add to (a) and (b) a third condition (c) so stated:

(c)   ... and the output y is produced by f and g in the same number n of time units;

Then, $f \approx_1 g$.

We can obtain stricter equivalences, in particular such as to allow us to capture the notion of *procedural isomorphism* between MoR. In this case we want f and g to be equivalent (we denote by: $f \approx_2 g$ if and only if, not only "they do the same things in the same time intervals", but also via "thoughts" that is step-by-step computational procedures, denoted by Pf and Pg, such that a relevant isomorphism i between Pf and Pg can be established. Hence, we can add to (a), (b) and (c) a fourth condition (d) having the following form:

(d)   ... and the output y is produced by f and g via two procedures Pf and Pg such that $i(Pf, Pg)$;

Then, $f \approx_2 g$.

In order to obtain this stricter equivalence we need a mathematical characterization of i, that is, of the relevant isomorphism. A valid method for addressing such issue consists in putting the computational procedures in a canonical form and *arithmetizing* them, that is, univocally assigning numeric codes to them, as a means to establish the relevant isomorphism between numbers or the corresponding numeric sequences. This strategy postulates the arithmetizability of the MoR and of their computational procedures - an interesting technique we owe to the genius of Kurt Gödel, which will be introduced later in this chapter. It is obvious that $\approx_2 \subseteq \approx_1 \subseteq \approx_0$.

4.1.2 Estimating the complexity of MoR

Our mathematics develops at an abstract and extremely general level, therefore in this book we chose to intentionally leave mostly aside issues of computational complexity. On the other hand, as the MoR capture the concept of algorithmic operator, we could easily import into the theory classical notions concerning the complexity of algorithms. Spatial complexity of MoR will have to directly relate to the ways these are implemented – thus to the amount of memory required – as the data structures used to physically realize them. At the level of the elementary cells of our digital universe, this spatial complexity should have a direct topological representation in the number and the disposition of the states of the cells whose configurations realize the MoR.

As far as the time complexity of MoR is concerned, given our assumption on the objectivity of absolute time, at the base level this will directly depend on the number of elementary operations required for a MoR to produce its output, or its action, given certain inputs. The number of these operations in succession, and thus the number of time units, will in turn depend on the measure of the relevant inputs or perceptions. Given an input i of size n, we will be able to compute the *worst-case complexity* and the *average-case complexity* of the MoR that think, that is to say, compute, i, on the basis of n, by applying well-known discrete mathematics procedures, such as big-O, big-Ω e big-Θ estimates.

In particular, it will make sense to state that two MoR are of the *same order* ("$\approx_\Theta$") when, even if they do not produce the respective actions exactly in the same time units, there exists a relation between the two which corresponds to the relation "$f(x)$ is big-$\Theta(g(x))$" between functions defined on natural or real numbers, that is: for constants C and k, when $x > k$,

If $|f(x)| \leq C|g(x)|$ ($f(x)$ is big-$O(g(x))$)

and $|f(x)| \geq C|g(x)|$ ($f(x)$ is big-$\Omega(g(x))$)

Then, $f \approx_\Theta g$.

This type of equivalence will lie at an intermediate level between the minimal equivalence $f \approx_0 g$ and the stricter one $f \approx_1 g$: two MoR f and g such that $f \approx_\Theta g$ will have the same order of computational complexity (e.g., linear or polynomial) on the basis of the elementary operations they perform. A distinct question is the one regarding *what* are the elementary operations precisely, and, as we will see, this is a topic on which recursion theory has something to say.

4.2 Partial and inverse MoR

By a *partial model of reference* we mean a MoR that, for some perceptions, does not produce any action. There are good reasons to affirm the existence of partial MoR. In our present context, which is the mathematics of the MoR, in order to convincingly show this it is enough to focus on the existence of algorithmic procedures that, for some inputs, do not terminate - do not deliver any output. The corresponding functional notions are given by partial functions.

Furthermore, in order to restate the classical recursion theory in its full strength in terms of the MoR, we need partial operators: the Enumeration Theorem of recursion theory, in its strongest form, states (we will examine it later on) that there exists a universal recursive operator that generates all the recursive operators of any number of inputs. We can stress the correspondence between the latter and the universal Turing machine, this being a Turing machine capable of computing a universal recursive function, taking the numeric code of any recursive function as parameter. Now, the universal recursive function has to be a partial function due to the Turing's Halting problem.

Thirdly, maintaining that not all MoR terminate their procedures of thought by producing an action for anything they perceive is consistent with the strictly constructivist, discretist and finitist perspective of our mathematics. To assume that there *exists* an output *for any* input of any MoR means, as we will explain later on, to make an intrinsically "infinitary" assumption. Hence, these remarks provide us with *a priori* mathematical reasons to state that there exist partial MoR (it being understood that a phenomenological study of our minds could prove very useful with respect to the question of partial MoR).

If that is how things stand, we need to correspondingly extend the various notions of equivalence between models of reference.

Given a model of reference f and perceptions $x_1, x_2, \ldots, x_n$, we write:

$$f(x_1, x_2, \ldots, x_n)\downarrow$$

by which we indicate that f produces an action when it perceives $x_1, x_2, \ldots, x_n$ (using the terminology of the theory of functions: it "converges"). In contrast, we write:

$$f(x_1, x_2, \ldots, x_n)\uparrow$$

by which we indicate that f does not act when it perceives $x_1, x_2, \ldots, x_n$ (notice that this does not mean that whatever instantiates the MoR does not think, that is, it does not perform internal computational procedures; rather, it means that the MoR does not converge to a determinate action following these thoughts).

Then, given any two models of reference $f: A \Rightarrow B$, and $g: C \Rightarrow D$, $f \approx_0 g$ only if:

(a) $A = C$ and $B = D$, that is the models are defined on the same sets of perceptions and actions;

(b) For any input or perception $x_1, x_2, \ldots, x_n$ (in this order), f and g

(b1) are both non-convergent, or

(b2) are both convergent and they produce the same output y.

... And the corresponding reformulation of $\approx_1$ and $\approx_2$ can be easily derived.

Following our discussion on the invertibility of the base rules of the universe in the first chapter, we also know that some MoR can operate "in reverse fashion", or more accurately, they have a corresponding *inverse MoR*. We can define the inverse model f^{-1} of a model f as that MoR that recognizes as input or perception what, from the standpoint of f, is the action or output, and that gives as its own output or action what, from the point of view of f, was the corresponding input or perception. Given a MoR, as we explained in that chapter, we cannot assume it has an inverse (it being understood that the MoR corresponding to injective operators are invertible on their image that is a subset of the respective domain of actions).

4.3 Recursive models

Our models of reference are a generalization of the notion of operator. In our intended model they "live" and operate in a discrete and finite digital universe, which was introduced and axiomatized in the preceding chapters: it is therefore wholly legitimate to import general recursion theory into the theory of the MoR. In fact, it is known that the recursive functions (a) are functions defined on natural numbers – hence, on the domain of discrete and finite quantities. Moreover, (b) on the basis of the renowned Church's Thesis, the computable functions are precisely the recursive functions. Points (a) and (b) exactly coincide with the two fundamental characteristics we have associated to the notion of MoR from its first intuitive presentation. This can thus be specified by making reference to some basic results of recursion theory.

Furthermore, through the application of recursion theory to the MoR, it will be possible to characterize in a rigorous manner the notion of *meta-model*, that is of a model of reference operating *on* models of reference – definitely, a notion of primary importance for the whole mathematics of the MoR, in particular in view of its general applicability to cognitive processes. And it will as well be possible to characterize that type of meta-theoretic operation which is *self-reference*, namely the capacity, possessed by certain MoR, of operating *on themselves*, thereby overcoming the rigid hierarchical distinction between model and meta-model.

What is, therefore, a recursive MoR? Generally, and informally, a recursive MoR can be thought of as a MoR which "refers to itself" in its definition and, thus, in its way of operating – that is, it is an algorithmic operator defined in terms of itself, or an effective procedure which calls itself. Slightly more precisely: a recursive MoR is a MoR such that its actions or outputs on the basis of certain perceptions or inputs can be determined by the outputs or actions of that same MoR with respect to *simpler* inputs or perceptions: what a recursive MoR does for certain more complex perceptions depends on what *it itself* does, or would do, for simpler perceptions (where "simpler" can in turn be characterized in a mathematically precise manner, as we will see shortly). A recursive MoR can therefore be presented by a formal definition having a particular structure: in a recursive definition, the operator introduced in the *definiendum* appears, i.e. recurs, in the *definiens*.

There exist theories of computational mathematics alternative to recursion, such as Church's λ-calculus, Markovian algorithms, etc. But, firstly, they all are demonstrably equivalent to recursion theory. Moreover, in the second place, the recursive approach has the significant advantage that, by means of it, we can present the set of operators by starting from some elementary operators or MoR, and introducing more complex operators through recursive definitional procedures.

Obviously, this does not mean that the procedure employed is the only possible one – asserting this would be contrary to our thoroughly conventionalist approach. We will see that some operators or MoR introduced below using recursive characterizations can be re-defined in the presentation of the model-theoretic semantics of our formal language, as developed in one of the appendices of this book. For example, logical connectives and quantifiers, besides being derived through their characteristic operations, are inter-definable, that is definable in terms of each other, from a semantic viewpoint.

4.3.1 Perceptions, actions and numbers

Recursion theory is a theory of computability. However, computing is a process that essentially involves numerical quantities. Now, mental calculation is a type of computation; but not every thought or reasonining is calculation in this sense: how can therefore our theory be a *general* mathematics of thought?

The answer is straightforward: it basically lies in the consideration that today's computers already do anything they do (processing texts in several manners, recognizing speech, producing sounds from symbols, treating images, etc.) while being just arithmetic calculators, that is, data processors operating on finite and discrete quantities. This, as it is widely known, is due to the fact that many types of data such as words, sounds, or images are converted into numerical sequences via appropriate encoding.

In our approach, perceptions (the inputs), thoughts (the internal computations) and actions (the outputs) characterizing the MoR are state modifications in entry and in exit, that is to say, directed inwards and outwards. In turn, *internal* and *external* are notions characterized, as we saw on the basis of the definitions and the axioms of the previous chapter, as *relative* to a system, namely, a mereological aggregate of cells with certain minimal topological properties. To be precise, in our cellular model the dynamics of perception-thought-action that characterizes all MoR is an information processing procedure that corresponds to modifications in the physical states of the cells, which can be conceived as motion in different directions of active and inactive bits. In the strong isomorphism between physical and informational world distinguishing our digital universe, *the perceptions and actions of the MoR are already digitalized*, in the sense that they can always be seen as bits and sequences of bits (states of cells) in motion. The very notion of "input" or "entry" or "perception" for a MoR has a definite physical sense: it consists in the modification of states internal to a system that implements the MoR in question, following a change of state of parts of reality external to the system – and dually for the "output" or "exit" or "action".

If recursive MoR are therefore those that realize, at the physical level, the operations recursive functions consist in, that is, the actually computable procedures, then we can certainly state that these are operators from natural numbers to natural numbers because we are able to see the perceptions and actions of these models just as natural numbers, i.e., discrete and finite quantities. And there are several, totally intuitive, ways by which such correspondence can be established in a precise manner. For the purposes of formalization, the perceptions and actions of the relevant MoR must be presented as a system of *numerals*, namely terms that stand for numbers. As is well known, the set of computable, i.e., recursive, operators is not affected by the type of numerical notation employed: this is wholly conventional. We can refer to the number four by using "4", or 'IV", or precisely "four", or by writing four tallies in a row, ||||; and this changes nothing from the point of view of abstract computation, because the same conversion from one notation to another is a mechanical and effective process, which can be realized by means of a decidable set of conversion rules (for instance, rules implemented by a cellular automaton) – and hence, again, of MoR.

But what the numerals of the formal language refer to, in our intended interpretation, can be *states* or *combinations of states* of the elementary cells of our universe; and also structures emerging at a higher dimensional level, as long as the relevant isomorphism is preserved. In particular, we can see the sequences of active and inactive bits in motion in our digital universe as binary sequences of 1s and 0s. Thus, a sequence of bits in motion from left to right like this one:

...

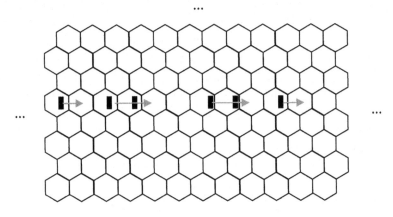

...

... can be seen as the binary number 1011001101. Alternatively, we can use a tally numeration system in unary notation, where a continuous sequence of active bits represents the number corresponding to the amount of bits; and an inactive bit functions as *blank*, that is, it separates two distinct numbers (slightly similarly to what occurs in several representations of the tapes of ordinary Turing machines). For example, a sequence of active bits in motion from left to right like this one

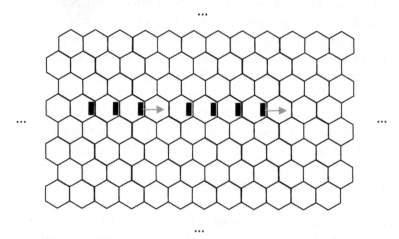

can represent the number 4, followed by the number 3, Alternatively, if we want to consider not only the positive integers (zero excluded), but the naturals (zero included), we can view the first bit of an active sequence as representing the number zero, and each subsequent bit as the addition of one unit (we will shortly ascertain that implementing the zero is not banal as it may seem). In this case, that sequence represents the number 3, followed by the number 2. As usual, in our perspective it all revolves around choosing in a clear manner the options of initial figuration, namely the way by which we "see" the computation in action, and then rigorously abiding by the conditions set forth. In this manner, any perception incoming into (and dually, any action outgoing from) a system that implements a MoR can be seen as an input encoded by a sequence of bits in motion; and such sequence perfectly reciprocates the physical state of the cells!

4.3.2 Basic recursion and the cellular universe

We now begin by introducing the basic recursive operations, that is, those from which it is possible to define more complex operators. In doing this, we will also provide some examples concerning how such operations are, or can be, actually realized in the digital and cellular physical universe that constitutes our model. To this end, however, an initial remark is necessary: in consideration of our conventionalist perspective, and the "fractal" characteristics of the mathematics we are progressively developing, we absolutely do not intend to maintain that the MoR introduced herein can be phisically realized *solely* in the way we described – that is why we have just said: "are, or *can* be". It is a peculiarity of our model to deem that computation is "in the eye of the beholders"; which means that any physical configuration that could sensibly be *seen as* realizing a certain sequence perception (input) / thought (internal processing) / action (output), by this same reason, realizes the corresponding MoR.

Let us consider a simple stone, for example. Although it might not seem so at first sight, a stone contains a huge amount of information and it can be seen as realizing a vast number of computations: an ordinary rock with 10^{25} atoms, taking into account the atomic structural complexity (angular moment, spin, etc.) can incorporate $\sim 10^{27}$ bits of information; its atoms are very active as far as exchange of electrons, generation of electromagnetic fields, etc., are concerned. But, obviously, many of these processes appear as scarcely significant and rather chaotic to us. Intelligence does not equate the amount of information and computation – on the contrary, it resides in the ability of *selecting* relevant computations and information *patterns*.

A MoR is defined by the task it performs: it is an arbitrary label assigned to a precise and deterministic sequence of modifications of the physical-informational states of the universe. This is why the same MoR can be realized at different dimensional levels, and by distinct physical structures, provided that "it does what it must do", that is to say, as long as the relevant isomorphism is preserved.

Let us bear in mind that the numbers, as we have just examined, in our digital universe can correspond to sequences of bits, namely of states of elementary cells with certain topological requirements, in various ways. As a consequence, in this chapter we can assume that the variables of our language L, employed to formalize the theory, now directly vary on what is realized by these *sequences of states* of the cells. Let us then start with the following basic operators-MoR.

The operator **reset,** r, given any input or perception (that represents the number) x as argument, assigns as output or action always and only one output that, from now on, we will denote by the asterik symbol *, and which we want to take, to express ourselves in algebraic language, as the neutral element (with respect to the addition) of the algebra emerging from our theory: $r(*) = *$. The sequence value of the operator **reset,** therefore, is $r(*) = *$, $r(1) = *$, $r(2) = *$, ...

The operator r corresponds, in our theory of recursive MoR, to that which, in traditional recursion theory, is the function zero. We preferred to introduce **reset** for several reasons; the first is that we precisely want to put forward as much general a system as possible from the standpoint of the algebraic interpretation of our theory. Now, a respectable abstract algebra in order to capture arithmetic will always have a neutral element (whose behaviour as neutral, we will see, is expressed by some operators we will introduce in short), but it is not necessary for this to be *seen as* the zero, although this is obviously not ruled out. Specifically, it is known that the semantics of zero (and the use of the symbol "0" as its numeral) is governed by rather complex conventions that, in our opinion, should emerge only at a higher and less basic level with respect to our ultimate "foundational" perspective. The ancient Romans, for instance, notoriously did not have a numeral for the zero in their notation. It is of Hindu-Arabic derivation, and it was introduced for technical and simplicity reasons: by means of 0 it is possible to have a notation which allows to line up the numbers and sum them rapidly, but an electronic calculating device, or a mind with particular computation capabilities, could well do without it. It is moreover evident that if "9 + 1 = 10" and "9 + 0 = 9", the numeral "0" has different meanings in these expressions: in the first it is simply a notational expedient to express a number in the decimal system, and an alternative notation is always at hand. In the second expression instead, the zero shows its function as neutral algebraic element; it is *only this second* function we are interested in, and we express it by our symbol "*". As a consequence, what suffices for our theory is precisely an operator such as **reset,** whose denomination is clear: what reset does is to *neutralize* (that is, indeed, to reduce to the neutral element *), namely to "reset", any positive numerical quantity "perceived" as input.

Let us now examine a first example of how this operator can be realized within the cellular model of our universe. Obviously, it would be extremely simple to implement this MoR directly in the cells, by inserting the rule *r* as a rule of modification of states over time. But it is easy to realize that this might imply a loss, for instance, of the overall *reversibility* of our universe at base level (according to the meaning of "reversibility" formally characterized in Chapter 1). A rule that simply resets any sequence of active input bits (which represents the corresponding number) in the sense of *deleting* it, thereby producing inactive output bits (in representation of *), would be a non-reversible rule, leading to a loss of information (if at *t*+1 the output of the rule is precisely *, this could be derived from most different inputs at *t*).

Instead, we can implement **reset** so that reversibility is respected by simply duplicating the input incoming in any one cell. We know from chapter 1 that any, even irreversibile, MoR *f* can be merged into a reversible MdR *g* with a greater number of inputs-outputs, assigning prespecified, constant or periodic, values to certain lines of input, and neglecting some lines of output of *g* (the *garbage bits*). And, as we know, when the number of active inputs incoming into a cell governed by our reversible super-rule is even, these are bounced back precisely on the basis of the super-rule φ- for example:

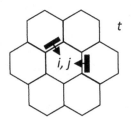 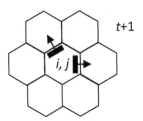

This means that, if we interpret each inactive bit as expressing the neutral element *, and sequences of adjacent active bits as sequences of tallies representing the corresponding positive integers, each pair of identical sequences converging on a cell from two different directions will be bounced back, one bit for each instant of time, thereby colliding with its image. The relevant output marked in the graph below is, exactly, constantly , * – or, more precisely, it is interpretable *as* *, once it is agreed upon that this (as is rather intuitive) is the meaning of inactive bits.

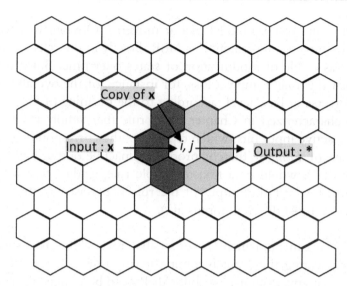

Furthermore, there is a group of n-ary operators or MoR, say p^n_i, that, hinting at recursive terminology, we can term **projection** operators. Firstly, consider a one-argument projection operator, p^1_1: given any one perception or input (representing the number) x, this MoR simply assigns that same number to it: $p^1_1(x) = x$ (therefore: $p^1_1(1) = 1$, $p^1_1(2) = 2$, $p^1_1(3) = 3$, ...).

We can see the MoR in question directly implemented in the cells of our physical digital universe, as it is plainly a part of our strongly reversible super-rule ϕ analyzed in chapter one. When the collection of active bits in entry into a cell at time t is odd, our cells realize that information transfer we labelled as "uniform rectilinear motion", (in fact, a suboperator of ϕ, namely the MoR *Perm*), and which can be conceived as an implementation of the MoR of copy unary *projection*.

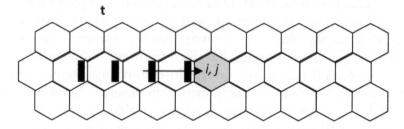

t + 4

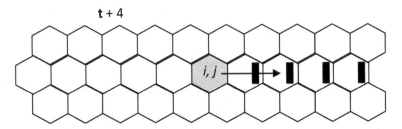

The cell $<i, j>$ has implemented the MoR **projection** p^1_1 simply by taking as "perception" or input at t a sequence of bits in motion representing, we assume, the number four, and at $t+4$ delivering in output that same sequence.

Besides, there are *two*-argument projection operators, p^2_1 and p^2_2: given a pair of numbers x and y as input, the former always assigns as its value the first of the two numbers, and the latter the second: $p^2_1(x, y) = x$, $p^2_2(x, y) = y$.[33] A good way to implement these operators in our model consists in embedding them into a double series of inputs in sequence, converging to a same cell from two different directions. We name these *A-series* and *B-series*: the A-series contains a a sequence of numbers: a, b, c, d, e, ... , expessed as sequences of tallies from series of active bits and separated by single blanks or inactive bits; the B-series comprises a sequence alternating sequences of active bits corresponding to the numbers in odd positions in the A-series and sequences of blanks corresponding to the numbers in even positions: a, [blanks corresponding to b], c, [blanks corresponding to d], e, ... The relevant output given by the cell is the one in exit from the same direction the A-series came from: it is a sequence that only selects the second element of each pair of numbers$<a$, $b>$, $<c$, $d>$, ... - that which is not "filtered" by the cell. In this manner, the cell delivers in output the second of each pair of numbers, thereby realizing the operator p^2_2.

For example, consider this A-series containing the numbers 2, 1, 3, 2, ..., which converges onto the cell $<i, j>$, together with the corresponding B-series, 2, [blanks corrisponding to 1], 3, [blanks corrisponding to 2], ... The cell, taking the input $<2, 1>$, $<3, 2>$, ..., will give as output the second element of each pair:

---

[33] It is clear why the operators in question are termed *projection* operators: in the analytical geometry encountered at school, $p^2_1(x, y)$ e $p^2_2(x, y)$ precisely correspond to the projections of the point whose coordinates on the axis of the abscissas and on that of the ordinates are x and y respectively.

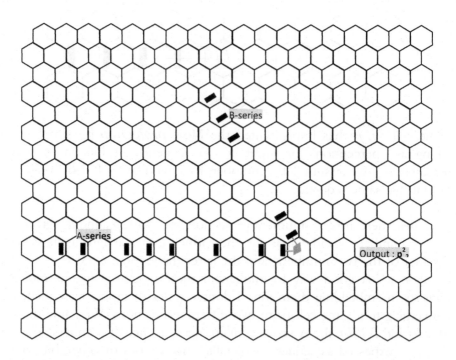

Now that the mechanism has been clarified, the generalization follows straightfordwardly: for each positive integer number n there exist n projection operators, p^n_i, with n inputs, which assign as value the i-th (the first, the second, ... , the n-th) of such input: $p^n_i (x_1, ... , x_n) = x_i$, with $1 \leq i \leq n$. For instance, $p^3_2 (2, 5, 1) = 5$, and $p^7_5(72, 4, 11, 128, 23, 8, 9) = 23$.

Another fundamental operator, termed as ***successor*** operator, s, given any one input or perception (which represents the number) x as argument, assigns its successor in the numerical series as its output: $s(x) = x + 1$ (hence: $s(1) = 2$, $s(2) = 3$, ...). It is a basic fact of recursion theory that operators of this type are computable (the theory itself is a mathematical formal characterization of the intuitive idea of computability). Anyone of us realizes the MoR in question – of course, at a higher macro-level that is distant from the elementary cells of the universe; and nevertheless, in an isomorphic manner, specifically because a MoR is defined by what it *does*. For example, when we "perceive" (whatever this represents) the number 7, and add one, what we do – regardless of whether we are aware of this or not – is to implement and apply the MoR ***successor***. Similarly, when we are given as "perception" the numbers 72, 4, 11, 128, 23, 8, 9 (in this order), and we run through the list until we retrieve the fifth item, namely 23, we are implementing and applying (what we denoted as) the projection MoR p^7_5.

The recursive functions are all and only those that can be defined, from the initial functions, through some operations in order to obtain functions from given functions preserving computability. This implies that, if some functions are computable, then the functions obtained by applyng the operations in question to such functions are in turn computable. The first two operations that are admitted are the following.

(1) The **substitution** or **composition** operator is essential in the theory of computation, and it is fairly uncomplicated: if f is an n-argument operator, and $g_1, \dots, g_n$ are all m-argument operators, then the following m-argument operator h:

$$h(x_1, \dots, x_m) = f(g_1(x_1, \dots, x_m), \dots, g_n(x_1, \dots, x_m))$$

is said to be obtained from f and $g_1, \dots, g_n$ by applying the MoR **composition**. Obviously, if these operators are all computable, then also h is – in other words, it is clear that the composition operation between operators preserves computability. The number of steps required to compute the output of h, given inputs $x_1, \dots, x_m$, is the sum of the number of steps required to compute the output (say: y_1) of $g_1(x_1, \dots, x_m)$, of the number of steps required to compute the output (say: y_2) of $g_2(x_1, \dots, x_m)$, \dots, and so on until we get the value y_n of $g_n(x_1, \dots, x_m)$, *plus* the number of steps required to compute $f(y_1, \dots, y_n)$.

However, some caution is needed in order for the composition operation between operators to preserve reversibility. As usual, this MoR will be realized at different dimensional levels and, at non-ultimate levels, it might result irreversible. But if such operator is to have a role also at the bottom level of our intended cellular model, we must limit its applicability in a precise way. In the unrestricted formulation of the composition operation, the output of a function can be substituted by any number of inputs of other functions. This means that, from the standpoint of physical implementation, we are allowing an arbitrary fan-out of signals. Now, we know from Chapter 1 that our super-rule ϕ effectively permits the fan-out of signals, but only at specific conditions: if signals split in one direction, for reversibility to be respected, they must always be able to rejoin in the inverse direction. As a consequence, at elementary level the composition of operators must be restricted to the case of one-to-one composition, that is to say the composition implying a one-to-one substitution of the output variables with input variables. Notwithstanding this, the general composition operation schema is however the one above.

(2) The (***primitive***) ***recursion*** operator is the following: if f is an n-argument operator, and g is an $n + 2$ argument operator, then the $n + 1$ argument operator h so specified:

(i) $h(x_1, \dots, x_n, *) = f(x_1, \dots, x_n)$
(ii) $h(x_1, \dots, x_n, s(x)) = g(x_1, \dots, x_n, x, h(x_1, \dots, x_n, x))$

is said to be obtained via (primitive) recursion from f and g.

Recursion is a kind of mathematical induction, which realizes in precise terms the intuitive idea according to which a MoR can "call itself". The strategy builds on the fact that (i) in the *base* of the recursive definition, the output of the operator given the neutral input * is defined; and (ii) in the *recursion step* of the recursion, on the basis of the definition of the output of the operator for a given argument x, the output for the argument $s(x) = x + 1$, namely for the successor, is defined. Now, if f and g are computable, certainly also h is: it will suffice to proceed "in reverse" with respect to the induction. In consideration of the clause (ii), the value of h in x can be reduced to that of its predecessors, that is of $x - 1, x - 2$, etc. Once we get back to the beginning, the value is given by the clause (i). Hence, also the recursion operation preserves computability.

4.3.3 Successive definitions of recursive MoR

By using solely our basic MoR, and operators of **composition** and **(*primitive*) *recursion*** we are able to define lots of derived operators or MoR. The forthcoming definitions will be expressed in our formal language L, and at times given in terms of (functors, that stand for) operators, at times in terms of (predicates, that stand for) properties-relations, to facilitate intuitive comprehension. Recall from two chapters ago that each property or relation (expressed by the predicate) R on any domain D is coupled with its characteristic operator $c_R: D_n \rightarrow \{1, 0\}$, in whose terms it is definable (and hence to which it is reducible); and, vice versa, each *n*-ary operator (expressed by the functor) f can be associated with the respective $n+1$-ary relation G_f, the graph, subsisting between the perceptions and the actions of the operator. Therefore, all the definitions in question may always be provided solely in terms of operators, or of properties-relations.

The MoR *addition*, *add*, is a recursive MoR that can be defined from the basic operators. The conventions regulating the operation of summing (natural) numbers can be the most diverse, just as the notation systems employed can be different. However, anything that may be considered as an addition must meet the following characteristics (it must be borne in mind that a MoR is defined by what it does): (i) by adding an algebraic neutral element to any number, one obtains that same number, and, (ii) by adding to a number the successor of another, one obtains the successor of the sum (here is the recursive element) of those numbers; this implies that, since the neutral element can be represented by the univocal output of the operator *reset*, *, the operator *addition* can be defined as follows:

(Df *add*)   (i) $add(x, *) = x$
              (ii) $add(x, s(y)) = s(add(x, y))$

It can be immediately acknowledged that such definition is congruent with the recursion schema seen above. In fact, it takes the following form:

(i) $f(x, *) = p^1_1(x)$
(ii) $f(x, s(y)) = h(x, y, f(x, y))$

with $h(x, y, z) = s(p^3_3(x, y, z))$: thus, the operator *addition* is defined (and therefore, derived) from the *projection* and the *successor* operators. Note that * has, with respect to the MoR *addition*, the properties required to a neutral element (by adding * to any quantity, one obtains that same quantity).

Just as addition can be reduced to the successor operation, so multiplication can be reduced to addition, inasmuch as it is just repeated addition. Regardless of what notational (and cultural) conventions are associated with the operator ***multiplication***, *mult*, multiplying a number by another is unquestionably equivalent to adding the first term to itself a number of times equal to the second term. We can therefore define multiplication as follows:

(Df *mult*)   (i) $mult(x, *) = *$
                           (ii) $mult(x, s(y)) = add(x, (mult(x, y)))$

Thus, the operation of multiplication, and hence the computation of a product, is defined (and therefore, derived) from the computation of sums (and * again performs its expected function, that is "resetting" to itself any quantity it is multiplied by).

The MoR ***rising to a power***, x^y, can be derived from the ***multiplication*** one, because like multiplication is a repeated application of the MoR ***addition***, so the rising to a power is a repeated application of the MoR ***multiplication***: rising a number to the power espressed by another is equivalent to multiplying the first number by itself a number of times corresponding to the second number. Therefore, the rising to a power is defined as follows:

(Df x^y)   (i) $x^* = 1$
                           (ii) $x^{s(y)} = mult(x^y, x)$

Thus, the operation of rising to a power, and hence the computation of a power, is defined (and therefore, derived) from the computation of products.

Along these lines, it is possible to recursively employ the previous definitions in a cumulative manner to obtain further operators. The ***factorial***, $x!$, is defined as follows:

(Df $x!$)   (i) $x! = 1$
                           (ii) $(s(y))! = y! s(y)$

The ***predecessor*** operator, *pred*, is the operator which delivers in output the predecessor of its input, or * if the input is *; specifically, it is defined as follows:

(Df *pred*)   (i) $pred(*) = *$
                 (ii) $pred(s(y)) = y$

The neutral element * is therefore the predecessor of itself. By means of *pred* we are able to define the **difference** betwen natural numbers, *diff*, which gives in output * if $x < y$, and otherwise:

(Df *diff*)   (i) $diff(x, *) = x$
                 (ii) $diff(x, s(y)) = pred(diff(x, y))$

Through *add* and *diff* it is possible to define the **modular difference**, $|\,diff(x, y)\,|$, which produces in output $diff(x, y)$ if $y < x$, $diff(y, x)$ otherwise:

$$(\text{Df} |\,diff(x, y)\,|) \quad |\,diff(x, y)\,| = add(diff(x, y), diff(y, x))$$

The operator **sign**, *sg*, equals * if $x = *$, 1 if $x > *$:

(Df *sg*)   (i) $sg(*) = *$
                 (ii) $sg(s(y)) = 1$

The operator **inverse sign**, *isg*, equals 1 if $x = *$, * if $x > *$:

(Df *isg*)   (i) $isg(*) = 1$
                 (ii) $isg(s(y)) = *$

Using **sign** and **modular difference** we can specify the operator **equivalence**, *eq*, which equals * if $x = y$, 1 otherwise:

(Df *eq*) $eq(x, y) = sg(|\,diff(x, y)\,|)$

By means of **inverse sign** and **modular difference** it is possible to define the **diversity** operator, *div*, which equals 1 if $x = y$, * otherwise:

(Df *div*) $div(x, y) = isg(|\,diff(x, y)\,|)$

4.3.4 Characterization of logical MoR via recursion

Particular attention must be paid to the specification of the logical operators. As we know from the first chapter, we can directly derive the (boolean) **negation** and **conjunction** operators from our super-rule ϕ for these are realized as merged in the rule itself that simulates them with constant inputs and output garbage bits. Yet, we can also (re)define such operators within the theory we are developing, as *recursive* MoR. In fact, given any property or relation R that can be expressed in our formal language, this will have, as it should be clear by now, its characteristic operator, c_R. Hence, the characteristic MoR of negation can be easily defined as:

$$(\text{Df} \neg) \; c_{\neg R}(x_1, \dots, x_n) = \mathit{diff}(1, c_R(x_1, \dots, x_n))$$

And given two properties or relations P and Q that can be espressed in our formal language and have as characteristic operators c_P and c_Q respectively, the characteristic MoR **conjunction**, $P \wedge Q$, can be specified, using **multiplication**, as:

$$(\text{Df} \wedge) \; c_{P \wedge Q}(x_1, \dots, x_n) = \mathit{mult}(c_P(x_1, \dots, x_n), c_P(x_1, \dots, x_n))$$

In such manner the conjuncion recaptures its usual meaning of logical product.

At this point, various options for the other connectives are available: for example, we can define the characteristic MoR of (inclusive) **disjunction**, $\vee$, by means of **addition** and characterizing it as logical sum; alternatively it is possible to specify it in the usual way through $\neg$ and $\wedge$.

The treatment of quantification results easy as well. Quantifiers were standardly introduced in the presentation of our formal language L. Now we can characterize them computationally in a strictly "finitary" manner, through characteristic operators –thus, again, models of reference – that in turn result recursive as well. To this purpose, we begin by defining the **limited summation** and **limited product** operators.

Obviously, summation as infinitary operation is not well suited to our discretist and finitist approach. Nevertheless, given an operator $f(x_1, \dots, x_n, y)$, we are able to recursively define the **limited summation** using the MoR **addition**, in the following way:

(Df Σ)   (i) $\Sigma_{y \leq *} f(x_1, \ldots, x_n, y) = f(x_1, \ldots, x_n, *)$

              (ii) $\Sigma_{y \leq z+1} f(x_1, \ldots, x_n, y) = \Sigma_{y \leq z} add(f(x_1, \ldots, x_n, y), f(x_1, \ldots, x_n, z+1))$

By the same token, we can specify the **limited product** $\Pi_{y \leq *} f(x_1, \ldots, x_n, y)$, by means of the MoR **multiplication**, as follows:

(Df Π)   (i) $\Pi_{y \leq *} f(x_1, \ldots, x_n, y) = f(x_1, \ldots, x_n, *)$

              (ii) $\Pi_{y \leq z+1} f(x_1, \ldots, x_n, y) = \Pi_{y \leq z} mult(f(x_1, \ldots, x_n, y), f(x_1, \ldots, x_n, z+1))$

Now, given any relation R having cR as characteristic operator, we can define the **limited universal quantifier**, $\forall y_{\leq z} R(x_1, \ldots, x_n, y)$, through its characteristic operator, $c_{\forall y: y \leq z}$, in the following form:

(Df $\forall y_{\leq z}$) $c_{\forall y: y \leq z R(x1, \ldots, xn, y)} = \Pi_{y \leq z} c_R(x_1, \ldots, x_n, y)$

Analogously, it is possible to introduce the **limited existential quantifier** by means of its operator, $c_{\exists y: y \leq z}$, using **limited summation**, or with the usual inter-definability with the universal quantifier. In such a manner, quantificational operators are always logical operations of limited summation or multiplication. On the whole, we can therefore define all the standard logical operators (or their finitary counterparts) by recursion, and assert that recursive properties and relations are closed under logical connectives and limited quantifiers.

We can further develop our mathematics via the quantifiers, defining operators such as **divisor, prime number, even number, odd number, quotient, exponent, least common multiple, greatest common divisor**, etc. Moreover, polynomial functions and integer coefficients can be defined as recursive operators as well. Since these successive definitions are routine, we will not present them in detail.[34]

We terminate this part of our analysis by introducing a third operation to obtain recursive MoR from known recursive MoR, that is, **minimization** – corresponding to the operation that, in standard recursion theory,

---

[34] See, for example, Boolos, Burgess and Jeffrey [2002], chapters 6-7.

allows to move from *primitive* recursive functions to *general* recursive functions. Minimization makes use of the well-ordering principle for the naturals: if there exists a natural number with a certain property, then there also exists a smallest natural number with that same property. As a result of the well ordering of natural numbers, this will be the least element in the set of numbers with the property in question, ordered by the less-than relation.

Hence, given a relation R, the so-specified operator f:

(i) $\forall x_1, ..., x_n \exists y R(x_1, ..., x_n, y)$

(ii) $f(x_1, ..., x_n) = \mu y R(x_1, ..., x_n, y)$

(where "μ..." is read "the smallest number such that..."), is said to be defined by minimization from R. And given an operator g, the so-specified operator f:

(i) $\forall x_1, ..., x_n \exists y (g(x_1, ..., x_n, y) = *)$

(ii) $f(x_1, ..., x_n) = \mu y (g(x_1, ..., x_n, y) = *)$

is said to be defined by minimization from g. In particular, using minimization it can be shown that if an operator f is recursive, then also its inverse f^{-1}, if it exists, is recursive.[35]

4.4 Formal representability of recursive MoR

We now want to make a technical digression for the sake of "formality". First of all, just in this paragraph we will distinguish between symbols of our language which are marked in italics, so far used to elaborate our computational mathematics, and symbols which are instead indicated in **boldface**. In fact, the theory of recursive functions we have just exposed is representable by systems of axioms formulated in the formal language L that we are satisfactorily employing. We are seeking for a formal theory which is capable of axiomatizing the computational arithmetic developed so far. In order to do so, its language needs to have the

---

[35] See ibid.

logical and auxiliary symbols we know, and the customary formation rules defining terms and formulas. As far as the descriptive symbols are concerned, we need an individual constant, "0"; two two-place functor constants, "+" and "×"; a one-place functor constant, the apostrophe " ' "; and a two-place predicate, "<", if required.

It results natural to interpret these symbols as signifying the number zero, and some recursive operators already introduced, such as *addition*, *multiplication* and *successor*, and the less-than relation as well. However, to be rigorous, we ought to make a distinction between these same operators (marked in italics, for example, *add*, *mult*, and *s* in the preceding treatment), and the symbols devoted to representing such operators within the axiomatization. In fact, besides offering an intuitive characterization of how the symbols designed to signify the operators performing such task, we will also provide a precise formal definition (as we will examine in a short time) of the notion of *formal representation* of recursive operators through the theory.

Nevertheless, we start by the intuitive characterization, to facilitate comprehension. The intuitive explication rests on the fact that "**0**" exactly stands for the number zero (however this may be physically represented by the states of the cells of our universe), "**+**" and "**×**" denote the *addition* and *multiplication* operations, "**<**" stands for the less-than relation, and " ' " denotes the operator *successor*. The fundamental syntactic role of the apostrophe consists in enabling us to construct closed terms within the formal language, that is to say, terms functioning as nouns, by successively applying it to the individual constant **0**. Specifically, in the portion of L expressing our computational mathematics there are closed terms such as **0'**, **0"**, **0'''**, etc., which are obtained by making the **0** be followed by the apostrophe for *n* number of times. Such terms are the numerals of our formal system. The bottom line of the intuitive interpretation of the numerals of the language L is precisely that they denote numbers – one and only one number for each numeral: the official name of any number *n* in the language is attained by making the **0** be followed by *n* apostrophes. Hence, for example, the name of the number two is **0"** – which is straightforward inasmuch as we know that we can univocally describe that number as "the successor of the successor of zero"; the name of the number three is **0'''** (the number three is describable as "the successor of the successor of the successor of zero");

the name of the number 1.470.515 is the numeral obtained by having **0** be followed by 1.470.515 apostrophes, and so on.

Clearly, if we had to write in full the numerals for large numbers in the language L, we would have to deal with a cumbersome notation difficult to handle in practice. Therefore, to make things simple, rather than writing the numerals for the numbers 2, 3, ... , etc., as **0"**, **0'''**, ... , etc. we could directly write them as "**2**", "**3**", ... , etc. (in case we need to write the numeral for the number 1.470.515, instead of writing **0** followed by 1.470.515 apostrophes, we would be able to straightforwardly write: "**1.470.515**"). Note that, anyway, this would only be a convenient "unofficial" expedient: officially, the numerals of the formal system are always defined as above.

As we provide the axioms of recursive mathematics, we maintain that these form a characterization of the intended model, that is, they work as constraints on the admissible models. While the mereological axioms formalized the ontological facet of our digital universe, those we will now introduce regulate the mathematical computational aspect: the configurations and sequences of states, which constitute the range of variation of the variables in the theory, *count as* the physical realization of the computational arithmetic in question solely because they satisfy the axioms. Also in this instance, our conventionalist perspective does not allow us to exclude that the axioms are realized also at a higher level with respect to the elementary one of the cells, and that, therefore, the notion of *computable finite number* may have further physical *realizers*. The essential point again consists in that the *realizers* "do what they have to", namely that the relevant isomorphism is preserved: once clear conventions on what counts as input, as output, as number, etc. have been set, *if* something complies with – for example – the formal characterization of the MoR **addition**, *then* that given something counts as a realization of the MoR in question.

Let us present two approaches by which the recursive mathematics outlined so far can be captured by a formal axiomatic system embedded in our formal language L. Firstly, we take the logical, descriptive and auxiliary vocabulary explicated above, as well as our rules of logical natural deduction calculus[36] in the role of formal principles of deduction.

---

[36] As we hinted at above, also other arrangements of the elementary logic will function equally

In addition to these principles, we can introduce the following seven axioms, which are the formal analogue of the Dedekind-Peano axioms for arithmetic:

(DP1) $\forall x(x' \neq 0)$
(DP2) $\forall xy(x' = y' \to x = y)$
(DP3) $\forall x(x + 0 = x)$
(DP4) $\forall xy(x + y' = (x + y)')$
(DP5) $\forall x(x \times 0 = 0)$
(DP6) $\forall xy(x \times y' = (x \times y) + x)$
(DP7) $\alpha[x/0] \to (\forall x(\alpha[x] \to \alpha[x/x']) \to \forall x\alpha[x])$.

(DP1) and (DP2) formalize the Dedekind-Peano informal principles, according to which zero is not the successor of any number, and distinct numbers have distinct successors. (DP3)-(DP6) are axioms that formally capture the behavior of the operators **addition**, add, and **multiplication**, *mult*, and, as it can be easily verified, they translate the recursive definitions, previously introduced, of these two operators, (Df *add*) and (Df *mult*), into axiomatic form. (DP7) is instead a *schema* of axioms, which employs metavariables. Such schema is the best possible first-order device to reproduce the principle of mathematical induction articulated by Dedekind and Peano, and whose informal formulation states:

(MI) Any proprerty that holds for zero, and such that, if it holds for a given number, it holds for its successor, is a property of all natural numbers.

Alternatively, we can adopt a second kind of formalization that does not employ any axiom schema (therefore remitting to substitutional instances), but it rather makes use of a given number of axioms. The axiomatization in question yields a type of arithmetic termed *minimal arithmetic* or *Robinson arithmetic*, often labelled as "system Q". Here we must adopt the symbol "<" for the minority relation – and the axioms are the following:

---

well, for all these systems are demonstrably equivalent to each other: they are all sound and complete, as they allow to derive all and only the logical consequences of the premises assumed, and to demonstrate all and only the logical laws as theorems. Hence, it will be possible to adopt a system of logical axioms (perhaps specified through schemata, with metavariables) and at least one inference rule (usually, the *modus ponens*); alternatively, a sequent calculus system; or yet another version. For our purposes this makes little difference.

(Q1) $\forall x(x' \neq 0)$

(Q2) $\forall xy(x' = y' \rightarrow x = y)$

(Q3) $\forall x(x + 0 = x)$

(Q4) $\forall xy(x + y' = (x + y)')$

(Q5) $\forall x(x \times 0 = 0)$

(Q6) $\forall xy(x \times y' = (x \times y) + x)$

(Q7) $\forall x \neg(x < 0)$

(Q8) $\forall xy(x < y' \leftrightarrow x < y \vee x = y)$

(Q9) $\forall xy(x < y \vee x = y \vee y < x)$

Basically, the procedure works as follows: we take the first six axioms of the series (DP) (corresponding to (Q1)-(Q6)), we remove the axiom schema of induction (DP7), and we add (Q7)-(Q9) that regulate $<$ adopted as primitive. Robinson Arithmetic is a rather weak system – its principal drawback is precisely the lack of the induction schema. From one standpoint, this does not support the appropriateness of Q as a formal system for arithmetic; in fact mathematical induction is a funda-mental method for the proof of lots of important mathematical theo-rems. Yet, from another point of view, it is exactly this that renders Q interesting: not having even one schema, Robinson Arithmetic is *finitely* axiomatized.

We can now delineate a formally precise explication of how systems of axioms such as the series DP or the series Q can formally represent within themselves recursive operators. To this purpose, we provide the following specification of the notion of *formal representation*. A k-ary relation R between natural numbers can be conceived as a set of ordered k-tuples of numbers. Then R is said to be *representable* in the systems of axioms in question, if and only if there exists a formula $\alpha[x_1, \ldots, x_k]$ of the language L in which the axioms are expressed, which contains exactly k free variables $x_1, \ldots, x_k$, such that for each ordered k-tuple of numbers $<n_1, \ldots, n_k>$,

(a)   If $<n_1, \ldots, n_k> \in R$, then $\vdash \alpha[x_1/n_1, \ldots, x_k/n_k]$

(b)   If $<n_1, \ldots, n_k> \notin R$, then $\vdash \neg\alpha[x_1/n_1, \ldots, x_k/n_k]$[37]

---

[37] Where the symbol "$\vdash$"stands for theoremhood (in the given formal system), or for the syntactic consequence.

where "**n**" denotes the numeral of the corrisponding number. Therefore, "$\alpha[x_1/\mathbf{n}_1, \ldots, x_k/\mathbf{n}_k]$" indicates the formula obtained from the formula $\alpha[x_1, \ldots, x_k]$, by substituting to the variable x_1 the numeral $\mathbf{n}_1$, by substituting to x_2 the numeral $\mathbf{n}_2$, ... , etc..

Hence, clause (a) of the definition of representable relation tells us that, if the relation R holds among the natural numbers $n_1, \ldots, n_k$ (in this order), then the formula $\alpha[x_1/\mathbf{n}_1, \ldots, x_k/\mathbf{n}_k]$ with the corrisponding numerals is a theorem of the axiomatic system. And clause (b) tells us that, if the relation R does not hold among the natural numbers $n_1, \ldots, n_k$ (in this order), then the negation of that formula is a theorem of the system. Thus, the formula is said to *formally represent* (by means of numerals) the relation in question.[38]

The properties of natural numbers consitute a particular case of such characterization. A set, say M, of natural numbers is said to be representable in the axiomatic system if and only if there exists a formula of its formal language $\alpha[x]$, containing only x as its free variable, such that for each natural number n,

(a)   If $n \in M$, then $\vdash \alpha[x/\mathbf{n}]$
(b)   If $n \notin M$, then $\vdash \neg\alpha[x/\mathbf{n}]$.

This implies that (a) if the number n belongs to the set M (that is, it enjoys that property), then the formula $\alpha[x/n]$ with the corresponding numeral is a theorem of the system; and if the number n does not belong to the set M (namely, it does not enjoy that property), then the negation of that formula is a theorem of the system. Hence, it is said

---

[38] If, instead, a k-ary relation R is such that the following holds:

$$<n_1, \ldots, n_k> \in R, \text{ if and only if } \vdash \alpha[x_1/\mathbf{n}_1, \ldots, x_k/\mathbf{n}_k]$$

Then R is said to be *semi-representable*, or *weakly representable*. Representability and semi-representability must not be confused with each other: if a relation R is semi-representable, from the fact that $n_1, \ldots, n_k$ (in this order) *do not* stand in the relation R it only follows that $\alpha[x_1/\mathbf{n}_1, \ldots, x_k/\mathbf{n}_k]$ is *not* a theorem of the system, but it does not follow that $\neg\alpha[x_1/\mathbf{n}_1, \ldots, x_k/\mathbf{n}_k]$ *is* a theorem of the system. The assumption that this follows for every R is equivalent to the assumption that the formal system is syntactically complete, but unfortunately (or not, depending on your point of view) from Gödel's First Incompleteness Theorem for formal arithmetic it follows that absolute syntactic completeness is unattainable.

that the formula *represents* (by means of numerals) the arithmetic property or the set in question.

A k-ary operator f is said to be representable in the systems of axioms DP and Q, if and only if there exists a formula $\alpha[x_1, \dots, x_k, x_{k+1}]$ of the formal language, containing precisely $k + 1$ free variables $x_1, \dots, x_k, x_{k+1}$, such that for each ordered $k + 1$-tuple of numbers $<n_1, \dots, n_k, n_{k+1}>$, if $f(n_1, \dots, n_k) = n_{k+1}$, then:

(a) $\vdash \alpha[x_1/\mathbf{n}_1, \dots, x_k/\mathbf{n}_k, x_{k+1}/\mathbf{n}_{k+1}]$

(b) $\vdash \forall x_1, \dots, x_k \exists! x_{k+1} \alpha[x_1, \dots, x_k, x_{k+1}]$.[39]

Having established these definitions of formal representability, we now turn to a fundamental result of recursive mathematics, demonstrated by Kurt Gödel in his famous paper on the incompleteness of arithmetic, and therefore also called Gödel's Lemma: systems of axioms such as the group DP, or Q, are, in logical-mathematical jargon, *sufficiently strong*, namely capable of *formally representing all the recursive operators*.[40]

Such demonstration is rather long and burdensome, although conceptually simple (so laborious that Gödel himself, in his renowned essay, presented only a schematic demonstration). In fact, it must be shown that the basic recursive operators are representable, in the sense defined above, on the basis of the axioms, and that the operations to define operators from given operators (composition, primitive recursion and minimization) never produce operators which the formal system is not capable of representing. We leave the detailed proof of Gödel's Lem-

---

[39] Clause (b) represents the uniqueness of the output of an operator, given the inputs. "$\exists! x$" is a defined, finite numerical quantifier whose intuitive reading is "There exists exactly one object ... , such that...", that is definable as follows:

$$\exists! x \alpha[x] =_{df} \exists x \alpha[x] \wedge \forall y(\alpha[y] \rightarrow y = x).$$

It is easy to show that an n-ary relation R is representable in the formal system if and only if its characteristic operation $_{\mathcal{R}}$ is: as a consequence, even when dealing with representability, we could speak only in terms of operators, or only in terms of properties-relations.

[40] See Gödel [1931]. It should be specified that in order for Gödel's incompleteness result to apply to the formal systems at issue, it is sufficient that they are capable of representing the *primitive* recursive functions.

ma[41] to manuals, and we instead examine some examples of formal representability of recursive operators.

The relation of *equality* between numbers, which we can denote by I, is representable in axiomatic systems such as DP and Q. This will be a set of ordered couples, comprising all and only the pairs of numbers $<m, n>$, such that m equals n. The symbol devoted to represent equality, in this interpretation, is the symbol of identity "=". Since it can be proved that, given two numbers m and n,

(a)   If $<m, n> \in I$, then $\vdash \mathbf{m} = \mathbf{n}$

(b)   If $<m, n> \notin I$, then $\vdash \neg(\mathbf{m} = \mathbf{n})$

we can state that the relation of equality between natural numbers is effectively represented in the formal system (through numerals) by the symbol "=".

Another example of representability is the property of being even, namely the set of even numbers. It is represented by the formula $\exists y(y \times 2 = x)$ (it must be borne in mind that "**2**" is an abbreviation for "**0'''**"), that contains only x as free variable. In fact, it is possible to demonstrate that, if P is the set of even numbers, given a number n,

(a)   If $n \in P$, then $\vdash \exists y(y \times \mathbf{2} = \mathbf{n})$

(b)   If $n \notin P$, then $\vdash \neg\exists y(y \times \mathbf{2} = \mathbf{n})$.

Also the operators *add* and *mult* can be formally represented precisely by the dedicated symbols. For instance, it can be shown that, given three numbers m, n and p, if $add(m, n) = p$, then

(a) $\vdash \mathbf{m} + \mathbf{n} = \mathbf{p}$

(b) $\vdash \forall xy \exists! z(x + y = z)$.

When we introduced the appropriate symbols of the formal language

[41] For example Moriconi [2001], in Bellotti, Moriconi and Tesconi [2001], pp. 190ss.

L, which would be needed to formulate the axioms DP and Q, we discussed the intuitive interpretation of "+" as expressing addition, etc. Now that we have precisely defined what it means that an axiomatic system for recursive mathematics *represents* certain arithmetic notions and operations, and having performed due verifications, we are allowed to state that + formally represents the MoR *add*, that = formally represents the equality I between numbers, etc.

This is a substantially relevant fact with respect to our conventionalist operational approach: rather than resting on an intuitive interpretation, one wants to focus on how the symbols behave within the formalism, or, in more precise terms, within the entirety of the theorems in the system; this in turn depends on the arithmetic axioms DP or Q and on the logical inference rules (the deductive rules we introduced two chapters ago). It is on this ground, that we can justifiably assert that "+" does what is expected from a symbol representing addition, "=" does what is expected from a symbol representing equality between numbers, etc.

4.5 Metamodels of reference

The notion of metamodel is in itself fairly simple: it is, roughly, nothing but the concept of a model of reference capable of perceiving models of reference, and operating on them or through them. The treatment of metamodels will enable us to import other essential notions of computational mathematics into our theory of the models of reference.

How can a (meta)model of reference operate on the models themselves? To address this question we need to introduce the fundamental notion of *encoding*.

4.5.1 The encoding of MoR

An *encoding* is simply another model of reference: it is an operator or MoR (that is, an algorithmic procedure), say k, which, given a model of reference f, univocally associates a certain *number* $n = k(f)$ to it. Vice versa, its inverse model k^{-1} (the corresponding *decoding*, which, according to what was said above, is in turn recursive, and therefore effectively computable), is a MoR that, given the number n as input, produces as output the MoR f such that $k^{-1}(n) = f$. The process of encoding and decoding allows us to associate numeric codes to the fundamental notions of our theory and, in particular, to the MoR themselves.

In fact, with respect to our cellular universe, the existence of metamodels requires that the MoR be encoded as states of the cells; these, as we have analyzed, are able to represent the natural numbers in various manners. A metamodel *will take as its inputs the codes of the models it perceives*, analogously to a by now familiar universal Turing machine that takes as inputs the codes of the particular Turing machines it simulates: in any computer everything is encoded in bits, and, specifically, the procedures are encoded in the same format of the data they compute.

Therefore, our encoding is a procedure of arithmetization, as everything is translated in terms of (positive) integers or natural numbers, thus, of discrete and finite quantities. Furthermore, such procedure is thoroughly suitable to our intended model of universe, because this, as we now know well, is a discrete and finite digital universe.

Several encoding procedures can be found in the literature on computability, and, for our purposes, it is not very relevant which encoding is employed. In particular, there exist many different and computationally equivalent arithmetization procedures, that is to say, many distinct ways to univocally and effectively assign natural numbers to operators or, in parallel, to linguistic expressions of formal languages and systems. However, a greater degree of precision is required: we need to be able to numerically encode the computations themselves that are performed by the MoR, that is, the thoughts by means of which the MoR elaborate the respective perceptions or inputs, delivering the corresponding outputs or actions. The encoding we will refer to[42] goes back to a clever procedure we owe to Kurt Gödel – together with Alfred Tarski, the inventor of arithmetization – who adopted it in the proof of the incompleteness of formalized arithmetic.

In its memorable essay, Gödel ingeniously exploited the Fundamental Theorem of Arithmetic, which states the uniqueness of the decomposition into prime factors of any positive integer: each positive integer

---

[42] Following that of Bellotti [2001], in Bellotti, Moriconi and Tesconi [2001] – but see also Boolos, Burgess and Jeffrey [2002], chapter 1.

(greater than one) can be written in one and only one way as a product of (powers of) prime numbers. This allows us to encode any sequence of natural numbers, summing up the information relative to such sequence in one unique number. Moreover, that very encoding is recursive.

Hence, given a finite sequence of integers – for instance, the sequence $w = x_1, x_2, , ... , x_n$, we can assign the following single number to w:

$$w = <x_1, x_2, ... , x_n> = 2^n \times 3^{x1} \times 5^{x2} \times ... \times n^{xn}$$

where "pn+1" denotes the $n+1$-th prime, that is, the number obtained by multiplying the first $n+1$ prime numbers, with the first one raised to the n-th power, n being the number of integers in the sequence, and the others raised to the power of the numbers constituting the sequence, in the respective order. Hence, given the relevant sequence number, we can univocally decompose it into prime factors, thereby retrieving the length of the sequence itself (determined by the first exponent) and the individual members (indicated by the exponents following the first).

The mere presence of numbers that encode sequences of numbers enables us to introduce an interesting MoR, the operator **history**, hst. Its usefulness lies in the fact that it allows to generalize the recursion procedure, not only defining operators, via recursion, by means of their value for the immediate predecessor or the immediately simpler perception, but also having the possibility of defining them via recursion on *multiple* simpler values, or even on all simpler values.

First of all, if f is an operator taking $k+1$ inputs, then, given $x_1, ... , x_k$ as parameters and x, we can think of the "history" of the operator f up to x (with respect to the parameters $x_1, ... , x_k$), as the succession of actions produced by f: $f(x_1, ..., x_n, 1), f(x_1, ..., x_n, 2), ... , f(x_1, ..., x_n, x)$.

Now the operator **history** for f, $hst(f)$, can be characterized as follows:

$$hst(f)(x_1, ..., x_n, x) = <f(x_1, ..., x_n, *), ...,f(x_1, ..., x_n, x)>$$

Next, at this point we can define f as follows, specifically via a recursion on the course of values:

(i) $f(x_1, \ldots, x_n, *) = g(x_1, \ldots, x_n)$
(ii) $f(x_1, \ldots, x_n, s(x)) = h(x_1, \ldots, x_n, x, hst(f)(x_1, \ldots, x_n, x))$

and if g and h are recursive operators, then also f is. A notable MoR defined through recursion on multiple values (two, to be precise) is the MoR **fibonacci**, fib:

(i) $fib(*) = *$
(ii) $fib(1) = 1$
(iii) $fib(x + 2) = fib(x) + fib(x + 1)$

… which gives us the *Fibonacci series*.

Next, codes can be assigned to recursive MoR by means of a recursive procedure matching the sequence of definitions via recursion previously introduced, and therefore the recursion structure itself. Inasmuch as it is possible to summarize into a single number entire finite sequences of natural numbers through the prime numbers factorization procedure, sequences can be directly assigned to the MoR (for it is known that these are always univocally codifiable), for instance, as follows:

$k(r) = <*>$

The code of the operator **reset**, r, is the sequence having as its only element *.

$k(s) = <1>$

The code of the operator **successor**, s, is the sequence having as its only element the number one. The following is a general encoding schema:

$k(p^n_i) = <2, n, i>$

The code of each projection operator is the sequence having as its first member the number 2, as its second, the number coinciding with the ariety of the operator, and as its third member the number i, $1 \le i \le n$, corresponding to the i-th input, which is returned as output.

Next, here is a schema for the encoding of every operator $h(x_1, \ldots, x_m)$ $= f(g_1(x_1, \ldots, x_m), \ldots, g_n(x_1, \ldots, x_m))$ obtained via composition from f and g_1, $\ldots, g_n$:

$$k(h(x_1, \ldots, x_m)) = <3, k(g_1), \ldots, k(g_n), k(f)>$$

Next, we have a schema for the encoding of every operator $h(x_1, \ldots, x_n, y)$ obtained via recursion from f and g:

$$k(h(x_1, \ldots, x_n, y)) = <4, k(f), k(g)>$$

Finally, we have a schema for the encoding of every operator $h(x_1, \ldots, x_n)$ obtained through minimization from g such that $\forall x_1, \ldots, x_n \exists y(g(x_1, \ldots, x_n, y) = *)$:

$$k(h(x_1, \ldots, x_n)) = <5, k(g)>$$

The encoding of the recursive MoR allows to apply Kleene's *Normal Form Theorem* to our recursive operators, this being "the theorem upon which the whole recursion theory is founded", for it "provides us, in the maximum generality, with a paradigm of all computational processes, namely a universal abstract model of computation".[43]

To begin with, we introduce the idea of the *Kleene predicate T* – expressing a relation that is defined on natural numbers, and used precisely to reduce recursive operators to normal form, and to represent computability in the formal theories of arithmetic. First of all, a Kleene predicate T may be intuitively characterized as follows: T conveys the information according to which a particular operator or MoR, which has been appropriately encoded, will perform a certain action (a certain computation), after receiving certain perceptions or inputs. To this corresponds an operator, u, whose exact role is that of extracting the relevant output.

In order to obtain the Normal Form Theorem, it is necessary both to encode the recursive MoR, and that the encoding be sufficiently effective as to permit, given a code for an operator, and an input or perception, an adequate simulation of the same procedure of computation, namely of

---

[43] Bellotti [2001], p. 129.

the thought that would be implemented by the MoR given that input or perception. To this aim, it is sufficient that the computational procedures, performed by the various operators, are put in normal or canonical form (i.e., a unique form which is conventionally established) and that recursive codes are assigned to these. In the literature, there are several ways to deliver such an encoding, thus, we can confine ourselves to address the reader to suitable manuals of computational mathematics.[44]

Normal Form Theorem: there exists a unary recursive operator u and, for every $n \geq 1$, recursive predicates T_n, such that, for each recursive operator f having a code e, the following hold:

(i) $\forall x_1, \ldots, x_n \exists y (T_n(e, x_1, \ldots, x_n, y))$

(ii) $f(x_1, \ldots, x_n) = u(\mu y T_n(e, x_1, \ldots, x_n, y))$

This means that "$T_n(e, x_1, \ldots, x_n, y)$" is nothing but the translation into formal, and computationally tractable, terms, of the fact that y is the code corresponding to a computation of the output of the MoR having code e, once it has received as perceptions or inputs $x_1, \ldots, x_n$. Therefore, $\mu y T_n(e, x_1, \ldots, x_n, y)$ singles out the code of the relevant computation, while the operator u provides its output. The theorem thus guarantees that the task performed by the recursive operator f can be reproduced by using the relation T and the operator u.

4.6 Partial MoR and recursion

We have already been talking of partial MoR, namel, of those operators that, given certain perceptions or inputs, do not produce any corresponding action or output. As we said above, the idea that such operators exist is in itself independently plausible. Adopting a functional notation, we denoted by "$f(x_1, \ldots, x_n)\downarrow$" the fact that the operator f is defined (that is, it converges) for the inputs $x_1, \ldots, x_n$, and with $f(x_1, \ldots, x_n)\uparrow$" the fact that it does not converge. Hence, the theory of recursive operators can be further developed by considering the existence of analogous partial recursive MoR, because partial operators allow to circumvent some of

---

[44] For example Bellotti [2001], pp. 129-136 ; Casari [1997], ch. 14; Boolos, Burgess and Jeffrey [2002], ch. 8.

the computational limitations to which total operators are subject.

One general reason to admit partial MoR is precisely our strictly finitist and constructivist approach to mathematics. Assuming that all the MoR are total, that is, they "act" in response to any perception (within their domain of definition) so as to deliver a corresponding output, equals assuming that there exists an action or output for any input received by a MoR. Yet, according to a constructivist perspective, it is not sufficient to generally assert the existence of something in mathematics, without this something being able, at least in principle, to be effectively *produced* or *constructed*.

Now, some operators may result recursive by construction, although, as a matter of fact, we are not able to specify what precise algorithmic procedure corresponds to such operators, and this underlying ambiguity induces us to regard them as somehow "suspicious". For instance,[45] let us consider the operator that could be termed **Goldbach**, *gold*. Our *gold* can be defined as the operator that gives as action 1 if Goldbach's conjecture is true, 0 if it is false. It is a recursive operator because, no matter whether the Goldbach conjecture is true or false, *gold* is simply a constant operator. Nevertheless, we are not able to identify the relevant algorithmic procedure and compute the value.

On the contrary, rather than introducing operators "in the abstract", without the possibility of indicating the relevant algorithms, we can instead define a constructively acceptable algorithmic operator, which is not required, for any perception or input, to produce a determinate action or output – that is, we can drop the assumption that such operator is a total MoR.

Let us examine, for example, the operator, say *pi*, which computes the decimal expansion of π. As it is known, π is an irrational number, a real number having a non-periodic infinite decimal expansion. Now, we present the following problem: Do there exist four consecutive 7s in the decimal expansion of π or not? According to the constructivist view we pursue, there does not exist something like a ready-made "infinite decimal expansion of π", since we reject the actual existence of infinity.

---

[45] The example is again taken from Bellotti [2001], pp. 140-1.

Therefore, the only way to respond to the question made above consists in *computing*. We start *pi* that computes the decimal expansion of π. If and when the four 7s appear, we halt and indicate that there is a positive answer to the question taken as input. Such procedure is legitimate as it is wholly deterministic, that is to say, at every step we precisely know what is to be *done*. However, what we cannot anticipate is if and when the procedure will terminate: it may continue indefinitely; or it may end, not because the output has been actually achieved, but rather for contingent reasons, such as a shortage of computational or practical resources.[46] In order to take into account this fact, coherently with our approach, it is sufficient to abandon the "intrinsically infinitary" idea that any MoR should conclude its task for any set of perceptions on which it is defined and deliver an output, and thus accept the idea of partial MoR.[47]

In particular, by admitting partial recursive MoR, numerous interesting results can be attained. Holding the assumption of **reset, successor** and **projections** as fundamental operators, we straightforwardly reformulate the operations of composition and (primitive) recursion. If f is an n-argument operator, and g_1, ... , g_n are all m-argument operators, then the following m-argument operator h:

$$h(x_1, \dots, x_m) \cong f(g_1(x_1, \dots, x_m), \dots, g_n(x_1, \dots, x_m))^{[48]}$$

is said to be obtained from f and g_1, ... , g_n by applying the operation of composition (and the left-hand side of the equivalence does not converge if at least one of the values of f and g_1, ... , g_n does not converge). Furthermore, if f is an n-argument operator, and g is an $n + 2$-argument operator, then the $n + 1$-argument operator h specified as follows:

---

[46] As to disclose the trick behind this example: the four 7s exist. They were found by Daniel Shanks and John Wrench Jr. in 1962, in the only possible way, namely after effectively *computing* π to roughly five thousands decimals.

[47] In the words of Hao Wang: "Gödel observes that the precise notion of mechanical procedure is brought out clearly by Turing machines producing partial rather than *general recursive functions*. In other words, the intuitive notion does not require that a mechanical procedure should always terminate [...]. Unlike the more complex concept of always-terminating mechanical procedure, the unqualified concept, seen clearly now, has the same meaning for [the constructivists] as for the classicists" (Wang [1974], p. 84).

[48] Where "$\cong$" denotes the equivalence between MoR as reformulated for partial MoR: f and g are equivalent partial MoR if and only if they give the same output for all the inputs with respect to which they *converge*.

(i) $h(x_1, \ldots, x_n, *) \cong f(x_1, \ldots, x_n)$

(ii) $h(x_1, \ldots, x_n, s(x)) \cong g(x_1, \ldots, x_n, x, h(x_1, \ldots, x_n, x))$

is said to be obtained from f and g via (primitive) recursion. Instead, the definition of minimization can be extended by admitting an unrestricted μ-recursion: given an operator g, the operator f specified as follows:

$$f(x_1, \ldots, x_n) \cong \mu y(\forall z_{z \leq y}(g(x_1, \ldots, x_n, z)\downarrow \wedge g(x_1, \ldots, x_n, y) \cong *)$$

is said to be defined through minimization from g (and $f(x_1, \ldots, x_n)$ does not converge if such a y does not exist). The Normal Form Theorem can then be easily reformulated in order for it to apply to partial MoR.[49].

Building on the new definition of the μ-operation, as well as on the Normal Form Theorem, we are able to treat any natural number e as the code of a partial recursive operator, namely that of the operator defined as $[e]_n$ the (n-ary) MoR whose code is e: $[e]_n(x_1, \ldots, x_n) \cong u(\mu y T_n(e, x_1, \ldots, x_n, y))$.

4.7 *Univ*: the universal recursive MoR

The first key result of the theory of partial recursive MoR is that it is possible to have a single MoR capable of emulating all the recursive MoR. In other words, we can now import the Kleene (Strong) Enumeration Theorem of recursion theory into our MoR:

Enumeration Theorem: there exists a **universal** partial recursive MoR, let us call it *univ*, capable of replicating within itself the thoughts of any recursive MoR. The MoR in question has the form: *univ*(e, $<x_1, \ldots, x_n>$). Specifically, it is that MoR which, given a recursive operator, $f(x_1, \ldots, x_n)$ whose code is e, namely $[e]_n(x_1, \ldots, x_n)$, takes as its own inputs or perceptions the code of such operator and (the code of) its input, and it delivers the same output as f or $[e]_n$ would produce:

$$f(x_1, \ldots, x_n) \cong [e]_n(x_1, \ldots, x_n) \cong univ(e, <x_1, \ldots, x_n>).^{50}$$

---

[49] See Bellotti [2001], p. 146.

[50] For a proof, see Casari [1997], pp. 369-70.

The MoR *univ* corresponds to a universal Turing machine. In fact, as is well-known, to any recursive operation there corresponds a Turing machine computing the values of that operation for given arguments. And a universal Turing machine has the capability of simulating the computation of any Turing machine: given a proper numerical encoding of any one Turing machine (the "program"), provided as data input in the same form as its other inputs, it is capable of decoding the program and of realizing the computation that the encoded machine would perform on those inputs.

In our case, *univ* can have the code e of any one recursive MoR $[e]_n$, in addition to the (codes of the) other inputs x_1, ..., x_n in its domain of possible perceptions; after thinking, i.e interpreting, i.e. decoding, that code e, it will be capable of reproducing the same reasonings as $[e]_n$ would have conducted on x_1, ..., x_n, thereby delivering the corresponding output in all cases in which $[e]_n$ would terminate. Herein, we discern another facet of that interchangeability between the physical (the hardware) and the mental (the software), embedded in our general approach.

The reciprocal of the (strong) Enumeration Theorem is the *Parameterization Theorem*, or *s-m-n Theorem*, which again we owe to Stephen Kleene. Moreover, it can be easily imported into our theory of the MoR:

Given two numbers m and n, there exists a (primitive) recursive operator $s_{mn}(e, x_1, ..., x_n)$ such that $[s_{mn}(e, x_1, ..., x_n)](y_1, ..., y_m) \cong [e]_{m+n}(x_1, ..., x_n, y_1, ..., y_m)$.[51]

In intuitive terms, the Theorem states that, given two numbers m and n, there will be a MoR capable of operating on the "source code" of a MoR with $m+n$ inputs – in particular, fixing as parameters the first m inputs, and leaving the others free.

Therefore, Enumeration Theorem and Parameterization Theorem are each other's counterpart: the former shows that (the code e of) a certain recursive MoR $f = [e]$ can always be perceived, that is, taken as input, by another recursive MoR (and, ultimately, the code for any recursive MoR can be perceived by the universal MoR *univ*, which is capable of replicat-

---

[51] See Casari [1997], p. 370. Notice that "$[s_{mn}(e, x_1, ..., x_n)]$" designates the operator whose code is $s_{mn}(e, x_1, ..., x_n)$, which is a function of $(x_1, ..., x_n)$.

ing the thoughts that specific MoR would produce, given certain perceptions). Reciprocally, the latter demonstrates that the perceptions or inputs of the MoR can themselves serve as codes; in computer science terms, the data of a program can effectively be embedded into another program.

4.8 Fixed point: recursive self-reference

One of the most noteworthy phenomena pertaining to recursion is recursive *self-reference*. Indeed, it can be claimed that a rough sense of "self-referentiality" underlies the recursive MoR as such: in fact, we have recognized that the crucial feature of recursive operators lies in the fact that they can "refer to themselves", or call themselves, in their definition. More generally, any *system* (in the sense defined in the previous chapter) can be said to be self-referential when at least one of its constituent parts is operating in relation to the system itself, so that its actions are determined by the status of the system it is a part of. Nevertheless, recursive self-reference is a more specific phenomenon: it can be characterized as the situation occurring when a MoR not only refers to itself, but besides, it is *aware* of doing so – thus, a system implementing it can, so to speak, become conscious of what it is doing by means of that MoR, through that same MoR.

Such expressions as "being aware" and "become conscious" can be interpreted as a form of psychological animism, and the fact that these are applicable to procedures, which are essentially computations, may appear anomalous. However, those expressions can be assigned a precise mathematical meaning, as we will now examine. We believe that recursive self-reference is at the ground of what is ordinarily termed "consciousness", the difference between conscious activity and any other thought crucially consisting in the fact that our mind, inasmuch as it is (self-) conscious, has the faculty of thinking itself – probably, subject to some operational limits to the capability of operating on its own "source code", but nonetheless able to possess a point of view on itself.[52] In our opinion, the realization of artificial intelligence is to happen through such phenomenon: artificial intelligence will be able to attain compelling

---

[52] For this point see Canonico and Rossi [2007], pp. 137-8.

results if the thinking machines we will construct are (self-)conscious machines, and, specifically, such (self-)consciousness will have to be a form of recursive self-referentiality.

In order to make this idea precise, we need to import into the theory of recursive MoR the *Fixed Point Theorem*, also called *First Recursion Theorem*, which is a key result of mathematical recursion:

Fixed Point Theorem: for every n-ary recursive MoR f, there exists a code e such that $[e]_n \cong [f(e)]_n$, that is, such that e and $f(e)$ compute the same operation: for every n-tuple of perceptions $x_1, \ldots, x_n$, we have that $[e](x_1, \ldots, x_n) \cong [f(e)](x_1, \ldots, x_n)$.[53]

To thoroughly understand the Fixed Point, it will suffice to conceive the recursive MoR f in question as an operator transforming a program into another. The code e we need in this case encodes an operator whose intuitive interpretation is the instruction:

"Transform the program of code $[e](e)$ according to the instructions of f, and apply the result to the perceptions $x_1, \ldots, x_n$".

Let us underline the self-reference in the definition: it mentions an operator whose code is precisely the code obtained by applying the operator of code e to e itself. There will exist a recursive operator of code b, that is $[b]$, which gives the code of this MoR as dependant on e, namely $[b](e)$. Now let us suppose that e is the same b, i.e. $e = b$. Given the definition above, $[b](b)$ encodes the MoR whose intuitive reading is:

"Transform the program of code $[b](b)$ according to the instructions of f, and apply the result to the perception $x_1, \ldots, x_n$".

And this is the code of a recursively self-referential MoR: a MoR that transforms itself on the basis of f, and applies such result to $x_1, \ldots, x_n$. This is a MoR such that its code, and the transformation of its code according the program f, are codes of the same MoR, that is to say, $[e] \cong [f(e)]$.

---

[53] For the details, see Casari [1997], pp. 371-2.

There exists a *Second Recursion Theorem*, which is often taken as essentially equivalent to the First; in fact, whether one is stronger than the other is a rather complex question, and here we can ignore it (the Second Theorem is sometimes referred to as "Recursion Theorem", perhaps simply because it is more well-known of the First):

Second Recursion Theorem: if f is an $n+1$-ary recursive MoR, then there exists a code e such that, for every n-tuple of perceptions $x_1, \ldots, x_n$, $[e](x_1, \ldots, x_n) \cong f(e, x_1, \ldots, x_n)$.

The fixed-point technique emerged thanks to Kurt Gödel who used it in the proof of its Incompleteness Theorem of arithmetic, and it was then developed and generalized by Stephen Kleene. In their application to our recursive MoR, the Recursion Theorems ensure we can define recursively *self-referential* (partial) MoR, in the sense that they encompass their own code within their own recursive definition. When this occurs, we have a fixed-point definition. Since, as is well understood, the codes act as the perceptions received in input by the (meta)models of reference, which are potentially able to simulate the procedures of thought carried out by the encoded and perceived models of reference, the recursively self-referential MoR are precisely MoR capable of perceiving themselves, and in this sense they are self-aware – conscious of the procedure which they themselves consist of.

A very primitive form of recursive self-reference, which is based on this structure, according to which a recursive MoR can retrieve its own code, can be recognized in the so-called "Quines" – small programs that yield as output their same own code. Every computer programmer knows that there exist programs that include modules capable of evaluating the performances of the programs themselves. We are convinced that a decisive step in the development of Artificial Intelligence rests on the construction of increasingly more "aware" programs, in the sense we have defined in terms of MoR.

5. Generalizations: Bits of Algebra of MoR

Now that we have incorporated basic recursion theory into our framework of the models of reference, it should not cause too much amazement if we assert that integrating other demonstrably equivalent theories into it, such as the lambda-calculus, or the Markovian algorithms would be fairly uncomplicated: as is well-known, these theories, despite starting from different underlying notions, specify the same class of computable operations. In fact, such an extension would not introduce substantially new elements to the knowledge so far acquired.

Something similars holds, we conjecture, for possible algebraic extensions of the theory. However, we deem that some points in this direction should be mentioned: a, broadly speaking, algebraic treatment of the MoR, such as the one very briefly outlined below, could lead us to some significant findings regarding these operators, beyond the sphere of strict mathematical algebra which, nonetheless, already has a high degree of abstraction and generality.

5.1 Algebraic characterizations of sub-theories of the MoR

We speak of "a high degree of abstraction" because, as it is understood, abstract algebra (unlike the elementary algebra studied at school) is largely independent from the particular domain of mathmathical objects taken into consideration. While geometry deals with spatial entities, and discrete maths and number theory are concerned with integers and their properties, abstract algebra is equally applicable to all these and other domains as well, for it relates to algebraic structures that simply are sets of objects with operations defined on them, satisfying specific properties, and normally expressible as equations. Hence, it is a branch of mathematics most contiguous to the formal logic that was extensively employed throughout our work, in consideration of its topic-neutral nature.

Given this preliminary characterization in informal terms, we should be able to recognize the link with our MoR: in fact, these are operators functioning over a domain of objects, i.e. the set of perceptions upon which they are defined; and they produce deterministic actions, as a consequence of thoughts or internal elaborations. Therefore, it is undoubtedly possible to conduct an abstract investigation of the MoR, aimed at identifying and defining their strictly algebraic properties. On account of our general approach to the mathematics of the MoR, such properties will be expressed in the form of *definitions* and axioms representing constraints to the interpretation, that is, on the model of the theory, with respect to the relevant MoR.

First of all, we can consider algebraically the theories of MoR analyzed in the preceding chapters, in a rigorous manner. Some examples. In algebra, a semigroup is defined as a domain of objects characterized by a binary operator, thus a MoR, say f, with the property of being associative, that is, such that, given any perceptions x, y and z it satisfies the axiom:

(Axi) $f(x, f(y, z)) = f(f(x, y), z)$

Now, we know that the syntax of our formal language L can be computed by a cellular automaton capable of universal computation, such as the one introduced in Chapter 1, and that such formal language can come with an operator-MoR we named **concatenation-L**, say *conc*, taking as input or perception pairs (sequences) of symbols of A (i.e. the set of symbols of the alphabet of L) and combining them. As *conc* is obviously an associative MoR, the ordered pair <A, *conc*> constitutes an algebraic semigroup (and in particular, a *free* semigroup).

Afterwards, we characterized the operator **composition** (employing some convenient measures in order to preserve reversibility) at the beginning of the exposition of our theory of recursive MoR in Chapter 4; inasmuch as these MoR are themselves defined over (the physical *realizers* of) our natural numbers, the set of all recursive MoR, being a set of endofunctions from natural numbers to natural numbers (let R be such set), in turn forms, together with the composition operator (let it be *comp*), a semigroup   because composition is associative: the pair <R, *comp*> is a semigroup algebra.

Furthermore, an algebraic structure such as a semigroup is termed *abelian* if its characteristic MoR (let it again be f), in addition to being associative, is also commutative, namely, if it is an operator that, for any perceptions x and y, satisfies the axiom:

(Comm) $f(x, y) = f(y, x)$.

In the first Chapter of this volume, we remarked that in the cellular universe the "active" and "inactive" bits of our cells, respectively designated as 1 and 0, are closed under the Boolean operators AND and OR, which can be implemented in every cell on the basis of our super-rule ϕ, from which they can be derived. Since AND and OR are both associative and commutative MoR, the ordered pair $<\{1, 0\}, \text{AND}>$ and the ordered pair $<\{1, 0\}, \text{OR}>$, specifically, constitute an abelian semigroup algebra.

Furthermore, we know from the last Chapter that in the cellular model appropriate morphological structures of states of the cells can represent the positive integers. Moreover, they form simple and known algebraic structures, considering that MoR such as *add* and *mult* are defined over them. For instance, from the very beginning of our analysis in that same chapter, we introduced the MoR **reset**, whose role is precisely that of "resetting" any perception in input to *. Besides, we can state that * does what it has to with regard to *add*, inasmuch as it behaves like the neutral element in respect to addition – for any number n, the following axiom holds:

(Neut) $add(*, n) = add(n, *) = n$.

When a semigroup contains a neutral element it is called a *monoid*; therefore the set of (the physical realizers of) the integer numbers with the operator *add* forms a monoid.

5.2 The MoR as homomorphims and isomorphisms: at the root of intelligence?

So far nothing new or particularly difficult has been achieved. A more salient fact than these scholastic characterizations is that some MoR can be qualified as possessing broadly general algebraic properties, in particular, as *homomorphisms* and *isomorphisms*. Let us consider a MoR $f: A \Rightarrow B$, and let us suppose that on the set A of its perceptions and on the set B of its actions certain MoR are in turn defined, say g and h respectively (so that $<A, g>$ and $<B, h>$ are algebras). If f is a MoR such that, given any perceptions x and y, the following axiom holds:

(Homo) $f(g(x, y)) = h(f(x), f(y))$,

then f is a homomorphism, i.e. an operator that, in informal terms, "preserves the work" realized by a MoR on a set of perceptions by mapping it onto the work of a distinct MoR on another set of perceptions. Next, such definition can be generalized to an arbitrary number of MoR that are thereby mapped by the relevant homomorphism. It should be stressed that the MoR qualifiable as homomorphisms are particularly important, on account of their capability of mapping not only inputs and outputs, but, more generally, *structures*. In pure mathematics structures of a given type are usually introduced together with operations that are structure-preserving, generically called morphisms.

Thus, let us assume that the MoR f in question has its inverse, that is, as we know, the MoR $f^{-1}: B \Rightarrow A$, whose perceptions correspond to the actions of f and vice versa. When f^{-1} in turn is a homomorphism from B in A, then f is an *isomorphism*, namely, a *bijective* homomorphism. It could be argued that the notion of isomorphism is a core concept of model theory.

The idea that there exist MoR characterizable as "isomorphic operators", in the sense that their task consists in bijectively mapping structures, can result of paramount importance for those who believe, as we do, that the MoR underlie our cognitive activities. Remarkably intelligent persons in any sphere of activity often are precisely those who are capable of "*seeing structures*" – hence, operations, hence, again, models of reference – where others see nothing but chaos, or magma, and of mapping structures to other structures so as to preserve relevant structural features. If our assumptions are correct, these cognitive capabilities are most likely to be strictly related to the activation of models of reference functioning as isomorphisms: those who possess them are enabled to map structures and (other) MoR, thereby detecting similarities and regu-

larities holding across possibly very diverse realms. Some, notably Doug-
las Hofstadter, have even conjectured that the isomorphisms, as
formations preserving information", are what produce *meanings* in the
human mind. A substantial part of our capability of recognizing meaning
in the mundane structures of reality, even where least expected, might
depend on MoR that are isomorphisms.

5.3 Passage

Beyond abstract algebra, we find the so-called universal algebra, which
studies notions that are common to all algebraic structures. In fact,
universal algebra (according to a definition formulated by Yde Venema)
is simply a branch of model theory: it is concerned with a certain type of
model structures, in particular, those upon which only operations, namely, no relations, are defined and in which the equational axioms are the
only ones used to characterize the operators. In the *Appendix I* to this
volume, model theory will be employed in a more general and robust
framework with respect to universal algebra, with a double purpose: (a)
provide a mathematical computational semantics for the formal language
L used in this book, and (b) expose a few tentative and preliminary
considerations about i-ese.

A1 First Steps Towards i-ese

I-ese, as hinted at some chapters ago, is the universal language whose development is one of the main focuses of the research performed in our laboratory.[54] Ideally, when Artificial Intelligence in a full-fledged sense will become attainable, the artificial-selves will primarily communicate by means of i-ese. The core idea of i-ese lies in conveying the semantic essence of concepts in an unambiguous manner, while at the same time preserving the undertones of meaning. Theoretically, i-ese should not only allow a quick transfer of knowledge towards machines, but also become, in the long term, an efficient communication tool between persons.

As a consequence, i-ese cannot be any of the natural languages such as English, French, or Japanese (although it may share some traits with each of these). What we already know about its structure is that this shall be built on the idea of model of reference. Its grammar will have to be centered on the sequence perception-thought-action, while phonetics and writing will perform the primary task of minimizing possible ambiguities. Some of the ideas underlying i-ese are already present in the mathematics of the MoR, as it has been formally exposed in this book. Let us examine a few of these, referring our initial approach to the framework of *model-theoretic semantics* and implementing it with respect to the formal language L adopted in this volume.

A1.1 Cognition and information

Model-theoretic semantics complies with some of the cardinal concepts of the transformational-generative paradigm of Chomskian linguistics. In their classical text *Meaning and Grammar*, Chierchia and McConnell-Ginet identify the following two fundamental Chomskian notions:

---

[54] This paragraph refers to materials from Canonico and Rossi [2007], ch. 20.

(1) "a grammar of a language can be viewed as a set of abstract devices, rule systems, and principles that serve to characterize formally various properties of the well-formed sentences of that language"; furthermore

(2) "generative grammars are psychologically real in the sense that they constitute accurate models of the (implicit) knowledge that underlies the actual production and interpretation of utterances by native speakers".[55]

As for point (1), it should be noted that the idea was already gaining ground in computer science and in mathematical logic even before the advent of Chomsky's cornerstone work. And, all things considered, nowadays "theoretical linguistics is a branch of (applied) mathematics".[56] In particular, our approach induces us to consider the generative grammar of the artificial logical-mathematical languages, such as the one employed throughout this volume, as a model serving as a starting point in the study of the grammars of natural languages, like Italian, English, or Japanese.

With respect to point (2), it is a renowned fact that the idea of referentialist semantics, i.e. of semantics as a systematic connection between linguistic entities and mundane entities, is a focus of objection from the syntacticists led by Chomsky. However, by this time it should be clear that our research approach rests on an isomorphism between physical reality and informational reality (hence, between "world" and "mind") such that it allows to set aside some traditional distinctions: affirming that everything is physical or hardware, and maintaining that everything is mental or software, is equivalent to drawing two general schemes of description of a unique reality.

Specifically, we conjecture that, besides constituting a valid mathematical model of the reality surrounding us, the formalization of the mathematics of the MoR involves mental realization in a precise sense: we deem it plausible that any speaker of a language comparable to natural languages should have, realized in the mind, a structure that is not very different from the one we have partly investigated. As is probably clear by now, what we mean by "realized in the mind" is that it will have to

---

[55] Chierchia and McConnell-Ginet [1990], pp. 1-2.
[56] Ibid.

implement a structure of *models of reference*, which is largely isomorphic to the one we have described in mathematical terms. If, according to Montague, model-theoretic semantics is a branch of (applied) mathematics, and in Chomsky's view, grammar is based on cognitive structures, we think that the path towards i-ese progresses through a close connection between the two approaches: precisely, in the systematic connection between generative linguistics and the methods of modern logical semantics – in particular, as developed in the model-theoretic semantics and in the *Montague grammar*.[57] As we will now discuss in detail, the key of our semantic proposal lies in treating the MoR themselves as the *meanings*, in a computational sense, of the linguistic expressions; and such move is precisely an attempt at unifying the two aforementioned perspectives.

We need to ask ourselves what *constraints* should, more specifically, be imposed on the syntax and the semantics of a language possessing the computational characteristics of implementability and learnability such as those we are seeking?

A first requirement that *must* be met unconditionally can be labelled as "computability of meanings": the amazing complexity of languages must be assimilable to a finite set of *primitive* structures, with the addition of instructions to modify them and *recursively* create new ones. Donald Davidson, notoriously, asserted that the grammar of any language learnable by a finite cognitive agent must respect precise finiteness requirements[58] – in particular, it must be producible by a grammar encoded in a decidable set of rules. The point here is to explain that we understand (namely, we assign the "right" meaning to) potentially infinite unheard-of linguistic expressions, as long as they are "grammatical", i.e. syntactically well-formed. It is a noted fact that Noam Chomsky himself has never ceased to draw the attention to this aspect. As Wittgenstein states in

---

[57] In his most remarkable article, *The Proper Treatment of Quantification in Ordinary English*, Montague constructs a formal language that is analogous to the one presented hereinafter, and he mathematically characterizes its semantics in a recursive manner (as we will do as well). Then he shows how progressively more extended fragments of ordinary language (English, in this instance) can be translated into formalism: see Montague [1974].

[58] "In contrast to shaky hunches about how we learn language, I propose what seems to me clearly to be a necessary feature of a learnable language: it must be possible to give a constructive account of the meaning of the sentences in the language. Such an account I call a theory of meaning for the language, and I suggest that a theory of meaning that conflicts with this condition, whether put forward by philosopher, linguist or psychologist, cannot be a theory of a natural language; and if it ignores this condition, it fails to deal with something central to the concept of a language" (Davidson [1984], p. 47).

Tractatus logico-philosophicus: "we understand the sense of a propositional sign without its having been explained to us" (4.02), and "it belongs to the essence of a proposition that it should be able to communicate a *new* sense to us" (4.027).

We argue that the only possible explanation for this fact is in terms of a computation of the semantic value of every expression starting with a finite number of constituents that are to be already known: "a proposition must use old expressions to comunicate a new sense" (4.03). We know the meaning of a finite number of simple expressions, and we have an algorithm to derive the meaning of the compounds from their constituents: "the meanings of simple signs (words) must be explained to us if we are to understand them. With propositions, however, we make ourselves understood" (4.026).[59]

The formalization we will expose below thoroughly meets these computational requirements. In fact, it includes the identification of operators, hence MoR, assigning meanings to the simple expressions of the language; and it specifies what operators, hence MoR, constitute algorithms to obtain the meanings of complex expressions from their components. Such algorithms should work recursively. Therefore, the semantics proposed can be implemented by a discrete states machine, such as a universal Turing machine, and, most noticeably, as a cellular automaton capable of universal computation.

The second requisite condition with trespect to i-ese can be satisfied to different degrees, however the mathematics of the MoR represents a valid theoretical basis to fulfil it with increasing accuracy. Here, we are referring to the requirement of "semantic universality" whose essential idea is the following: human beings (and the future artificial selves delivered by artificial intelligence) must have not only the syntactic structures, but also the semantic concepts instantiated in the hardware-brain.

This particular idea has some contemporary antecedents. The research program of generative linguistics assumes that there exist some fundamental linguistic structures that can be recognized in any language, regardeless of the differences between one language and another, and thus inherent to the specificity of *the* human language as such. Our analysis,

---

[59] See Wittgenstein [1921], pp. 44-45.

directed to i-ese, rests on a strict parallelism between syntax and semantics also on this – which implies that to universal syntactic structures
there shall correspond a set of universally available semantic notions
that, in principle, we must be able to detect in any human language (for
instance, we could refer to the so-called *thematic roles* that were classically
introduced by Fillmore). Such notions as **agent, cause, change, goal,
origin** (which we would call models of reference!) are good candidates
for concepts that could be employed in any inter-linguistic generalization.

Some scholars even maintain that languages differ, from the point of
view of semantics, primarily at lexical level: the peculiarities of lexicon
are what children must learn first of all; by contrast, combinatory principles for lexical units are very general and recurrent. Considerably,
Chomsky argued that, in order for a child learner to be able to acquire a
language, his mind must be endowed with innate devices that a priori
determine the grammatical structures: "the concepts are already available,
with much or all of their intricacy and stucture predetermined, and [...]
the child's task is to assign labels to concepts".[60]

A language such as i-ese should be able to convey – or, at least, to provide a tool to better express – semantic universals. For instance, we do
not have knowledge of any language not containing operators – hence,
MoR – that correspond to the boolean extensional **conjunction**, the
enunciative **negation**, etc. Furthermore, i-ese will have to reflect the
inescapable predicative structure of language. As we have briefly seen a
few chapters ago, predication might be a candidate *par excellence* for the
role of semantic universal, because, as Chierchia and McConnell-Ginet
make clear, languages are not limited to additive principles like conjunction: predication seems to be ubiquitous as well,[61] as a structure traceable
in any human language we know.

There exists a long-standing tradition of studies on language in accordance to which it is necessary to distinguish different semantic aspects in
the meaning of linguistic expressions (from the medieval distinction
between *intensio* and *comprehensio*, to the Fregean division between *Sinn*
and *Bedeutung*, to that between *signification* and *signifié* formulated by Fer-

---

60 Chomsky [1992], p. 113.
61 See Chierchia and McConnell-Ginet [1993], p. 13.

dinand de Saussure, up to the present – nonetheless having ancient roots – categories of intension and extension). In particular, traditionally, a distinction has been operated between two facets of meaning in correspondence to two fundamental features of language in general:

(1) *Informative aspect*: primarily, any language serves the purpose of speaking of the things of the world, thereby transmitting information. For example, in line with the classical Shannon definition,[62] the amount of information of a given message is measurable in terms of uncertainty reduction, namely the *exclusion* of some instances in a predetermined field of possibilities. This is exactly what we commonly do by asserting simple, ordinary statements. One who says "Outside it's raining" provides us with information because she restricts the domain of possibilities, by eliminating certain situations. Needless to say, one who tells us "Outside it's raining" certainly is not offering an exhaustive description of reality! However, if we trust the speaker, we can exclude from the realm of possible occurrences or situations all those in which it is not raining.

Moreover, such informative aspect of language is rendered possible because some linguistic expressions *refer* to mundane entities. The ability of recognizing the things to which the linguistic expressions of a given language refer is an essential component of the capability of mastering that language, that is to say, of being competent speakers of that particular language. In a nutshell, this is the level of *Bedeutung*: where the language *refers* to the world and speaks of the world.

(2) *Cognitive aspect*: on the other hand, remarkably from Chomsky onwards, language is deemed as also having an essential *cognitive* facet, based on mental representations that are manipulated by rules. Even though "Chomsky never devoted that much thought to the nature of mental representations, in general",[63] it is nevertheless clear that, in his view, syntactic structures of linguistic sentences are implemented in the mind, and that there exist rules operating on such representations. There must be cognitive structures "hard-wired" in the mind of a speaker, which encode her linguistic competence. The effectiveness of communication between the speakers hinges on their representations being sufficiently congruent, and activated through fairly similar mental processes (we can

---

[62] See Shannon [1949]

[63] Marconi [2001], p. 54.

mention Jerry Fodor's "psychosemantics" as the most popular among the works in this direction). From our standpoint, this can be nothing but a similarity between models of reference.

As it was correctly pointed out by David Lewis in *General Semantics*, this second aspect of language (that of the *Sinn*, we could say) is necessary, but not sufficient: according to Lewis, mastering a language cannot consist solely in having mental representations (whatever these might be) and being able to manipulate them, since representations, routines and procedures of manipulation of the symbols are things *having* meaning themselves: hence, mastering a language also implies having the capability of connecting the appropriate representations to the corresponding objects of the world they refer to. Concisely, also aspect (1) is necessary.[64]

We can combine the aspects (1) and (2) in a straightforward manner, taking into consideration both the cognitive aspects of language and the "referential" and informational ones, again by virtue of the strong isomorphism between physical and informational reality (therefore, as we underlined, between "world" and "mind") which inspires our approach on the whole.

And the key notion in this regard is, again, that of *model of reference*: the formalization we will present exemplifies the mathematical apparatus of model-theoretic semantics, preserving its structure and, specifically, designating the MoR as the meanings of all the main syntactic categories. Our basic idea is that the aspect of language, which is traditionally termed as "cognitive", plainly corresponds to the fact that a competent speaker is a complex system implementing a series of MoR within itself. Such MoR are the meanings of the expressions of the language (*Sinne*): they are operators expressed by linguistic forms, which (a) can be recursively combined, and (b) whose specific task consists in computationally determining the objects that are denominated by those expressions, or to which they refer (*Bedeutung*).

For example, what is the meaning of the name "Jacopo Tagliabue"? It is an operator, thus a MoR, which, on the basis of given inputs or perceptions, selects as output the object, i.e. Jacopo Tagliabue, designated

---

[64] See Lewis [1972].

by that name. And what is the meaning of the predicate "is a man"? It is an operator, hence a MoR, which, on the grounds of certain inputs or perceptions, selects as output the things that are men, thereby discarding those that are not. Being a competent speaker of the language equals being able to activate the "right" linguistic MoR to assign the correct objects to the appropriate expressions.

Here, our theory positively reconnects with several traditional cognitive and linguistic debates. Logicians and philosophers have argued for ages over the "senses" of words, or the "meanings" in broad sense, or the "concepts" expressed by words, and this is a long-established animated debate in philosophy and in science. The core of our proposal lies in the identification of these things with the MoR, and in the development of the theory of the MoR itself, which will enable us to ascertain that the MoR take many, if not all, the theoretical roles traditionally assigned to those notions: in sum, they do what *must* be done by anything corresponding to those notions; and that is why they are entitled to act those parts. [65]

Therefore, an underlying element of i-ese will be a strict adherence to what in linguistics and in logic is called the "principle of compositionality": the meaning of a complex expression functionally depends on the meaning of its constituent expressions. Notably, the respect of this principle is a necessary condition for having a language that is apt to be treated in wholly *computational* terms.

According to Richard Montague, one of the consequences stemming from this principle is the fact that there must be a strong isomorphism between the syntax and the semantics of a language that complies with it. Such isomorphism determines the fact that to different syntactic categories there correspond different semantic categories. To put it in terms of our theory of the models of reference, this means that expressions of our

---

[65] Let us recollect the four characteristics of the "language of thought" according to the hypothesis formulated by Jerry Fodor [1975]: the expressions of the language of thought have both syntactic and semantic characteristics, in particular: (1) they have constituent parts combining according to the rules of a recursive syntax; (2) their atomic parts must refer to objects of the world, and to their properties; (3) they are semantically compositional, namely, the semantic properties of complex expressions are derermined by the semantic properties of their atomic constituents and by the rules of composition; and (4) the expressions corresponding to propositional formulas have truth-conditions, and stand in implicative relations. As it will be shown, such requirements are realized in our formalization in a rather precise manner.

language belonging to distinct syntactic categories will correspondingly be assigned diverse types of MoR as meanings.

However, this is not yet a "theoretical-deductive" perspective. In accordance with the conception of reality presented in this volume, the grammar of i-ese should be founded on the MoR, in particular on a small number of primitive MoR from which all the others are derived. Nonetheless, i-ese will also be fostered by an inverse, more "empirical" perspective, focused on the study of human cultures and aimed at identifying universal semantic constants.

The following formalization rests on current mathematical logic and, specifically, on the formal semantics developed in the shape of Montague grammar, in line with what was justifiably argued: "presently, there exists no other method of semantic analysis which is equally rigorous".[66] Two characteristics of the model-theoretic approach worth stressing are (1) a perfect parallelism between the *syntax* and the *semantics* of the formalism – we will analyze such parallelism in short, and (2) the recursive computability of the meanings. In addition to these two features, we further include a third one that is peculiar to our research approach, and which involves the models of reference: (3) the MoR are the meanings of the expressions of the language, in a (traditionally) "intensional" sense; as we will see in detail, they are operators expressed by the linguistic forms, which (a) can be recursively combined, and (b) whose specific task consists in computationally determining the objects those expressions designate, or refer to.[67]

A1.2 Semantics

We will develop the semantics, again adopting as object language our formal language L, and, as metalanguage, ordinary English, supplemented with a totally ordinary set-theoretic notation. In order to attain a good degree of precision, careful attention should be placed in properly distinguishing between (a) the symbols belonging to the object language

---

[66] Casalegno [1997], p. 174.

[67] Henceforth, we will normally say that a linguistic expression *expresses* a certain MoR, and that it designates the type of object determined by the operating of that MoR.

L, that is, the formal language *whose* semantics will now be exposed, and (b) those pertaining to the informal metalanguage *through which* the semantics for the object language is exposed. To this purpose, we will employ **boldface fonts** to denote the latter, and these only (this should not be confused with the use of boldfaced italics fonts carried out in the rest of the book for the expressions that refer to the MoR, or for other purposes).

A1.2.1 Formal model

An *interpretation* or *model* M of the formal language L is an assignment of meanings to the expressions of L in a certain *structure* S. Precisely, a model is an ordered pair constituted of the structure and an operator v, i.e. M = <S, v>. A structure S is in turn an ordered n-tuple, S = <**S, T, <, D, W, @**>.

The description of the model M is the following: **S** is a finite set of *points* of space: $s_1, \ldots, s_n$. Each point **s** is an ordered triple, namely **s** = <**i, j, k**>, where **i, j, k** are its spatial coordinates. Hence, **S** effectively is a set of ordered triples **S** = **I** × **J** × **K**, where **I**, **J** and **K** are the sets of coordinates.

T is the set of the *instants* of time: $t_1, \ldots, t_n$.

< is an *order relation* defined on **T**. Given any two instants **t**, t_1 ∈ **T**, "**t** < t_1" says that the instant **t** precedes the instant t_1. In consonance with the discussion conducted in the introduction, we know that the relation **<** will be a discrete, strict linear order (as we do not admit the existence of the temporal continuum), specifically, it will satisfy the following conditions:

(a) given any one instant **t**, it is not the case that **t** < **t**;
(b) given any two instants **t**, t_1 ∈ **T**: either **t** < t_1 , or **t** = t_1, or t_1 < **t**;
(c) given any three instants **t**, t_1, t_2 ∈ **T**: if **t** < t_1 and t_1 < t_2, then **t** < t_2.

D is a finite set of *objects* (it is also called the *domain* of the structure S, and therefore of the model M). This is the set of the things of the world: the things that exist in S and, thus, in M. Referring to the intended model of our computational universe, this means: the set of the cells and of the aggregates of cells.

We also know that, assuming the idea of absolute space and time, each cell can be identified as an ordered pair. For any cell c, $c = <s, t>$, where s is the relevant point of space, and t the instant of time. In turn, s is an ordered triple $s = <i, j, k>$, hence, altogether $c = <<i, j, k>, t>$.

However, D is not only composed of cells, but also, precisely of aggregates of cells. The mereological axioms, which were introduced in Chapter 3 using our formal language L, determine in exact terms what aggregates, and therefore, what objects, exist. These axioms, as we know, specifically function as constraints on the set of admissible models.

W is a finite set of *situations*: w_1, ... , w_n. A situation $w \in W$ is a certain instantaneous distribution of properties on the objects of the domain. In reference to the intended model, this signifies: a certain distribution of states on the cells, that is, a certain possible configuration of the universe at a given instant. Nevertheless, a situation is not merely a configuration of the cells with respect to the states; but rather it is also a configuration of all the objects of the universe (i.e. the aggregates of cells) with regard to the properties emerging at all levels from the distribution of the states on the cells.

$@ \in W$ is the *present* situation. This is a particular designated situation, namely the overall configuration of the universe at the current instant of time.

We add the following notion that is derived from those explicitly included in the structure S: $C = W \times T$ is a set of *circumstances*. Thus, the set of the circumstances is the set of ordered pairs of situations and instants of time.

v is a *semantic* or *interpretation* operator. Such operator recursively assigns meanings to the expressions of our formal language. The mode of operating of v is at the core of the semantic formalism.

Finally, we need a distinct operator from v – let it be a – specifically assigning values to the individual *variables* of L, that is to say, mapping each variable v of L onto an object d of the domain, i.e. on an object d

∈ **D**. In some model-theoretic frameworks, the assignment of values to the variables is relativized to circumstances, or to both circumstances and times. This would introduce a few theoretical complexities we prefer to avoid here. The semantic role of **a** will be explained shortly.

A1.2.2 Tarskian semantics via recursion

The functioning of **v** is again defined recursively.

First of all, the operator assigns a meaning to the *descriptive constant* symbols of L, according to the following clauses:

If c is a noun or individual constant of L, then

$$\mathbf{v}(c) = \mathbf{c}\colon \mathbf{W} \times \mathbf{T} \to \mathbf{D}.$$

If f is a functor or n-ary constant funtor of L, then

$$\mathbf{v}(f) = \mathbf{k}\colon \mathbf{W} \times \mathbf{T} \to \mathbf{F} = \{\mathbf{f} \mid \mathbf{f}\colon \mathbf{D}^n \to \mathbf{D}\}.$$

If P is a predicate or n-ary predicate constant of L, then

$$\mathbf{v}(P) = \mathbf{p}\colon \mathbf{W} \times \mathbf{T} \to \mathbf{P}^n \subseteq \mathbf{D}^n.$$

Where:

c is an operator from circumstances (pairs <situation, instant of time>) to objects in **D**: for each $\mathbf{w} \in \mathbf{W}$ and $\mathbf{t} \in \mathbf{T}$, $\mathbf{v}(c)(<\mathbf{w}, \mathbf{t}>) \in \mathbf{D}$.

k is an operator from circumstances to operators from n-tuples of objects in **D** to objects in **D**: for each $\mathbf{w} \in \mathbf{W}$ and $\mathbf{t} \in \mathbf{T}$, $\mathbf{v}(f)(<\mathbf{w}, \mathbf{t}>) \in \mathbf{F}$.

p is an operator from circumstances to subsets of the set of n-tuples of objects in **D**: for each $\mathbf{w} \in \mathbf{W}$ and $\mathbf{t} \in \mathbf{T}$, $\mathbf{v}(P)(<\mathbf{w}, \mathbf{t}>) \subseteq \mathbf{D}^n$.

The operation carried out by **v** can be explained as follows: **c**, **f** and **p** are different types of *models of reference*, which are assigned by **v** as meanings of, respectively, nouns or individual constants, functors, and predicates or predicate constants. These MoR, as we mentioned in the inary informal description at the beginning of this chapter, are the meanings of the corresponding expressions of L, because they computationally determine the different objects those expressions designate, or refer to.

Clause n. 1 tells us that a noun c of the language L expresses an operator, or MoR, **c** that, given the perception of a certain circumstance, produces as output the object designated by c in that specific circumstance, namely in that situation and at that time. For instance, if c = "Jacopo Tagliabue" (i.e. assuming that the proper noun c of L translates the noun "Jacopo Tagliabue" of ordinary language), the corresponding MoR **c** is the operator that, among the objects of its domain of possible perceptions, properly selects the individual Jacopo Tagliabue as the bearer, or referent, of that name. Being able to use the noun c, that is, mastering its meaning, equals knowing what object is denoted by such noun; specifically, it is equivalent to being endowed with the MoR that, having "perceived" certain circumstances, yields as output the right object.

Clause n. 2 specifies that a constant functor f of L expresses an operator **k** that, after perceiving a certain circumstance, gives as output the operator **f** taken from a set **F** of operators defined on **D** (precisely, an operator from n-tuples of objects of the domain to objects of the domain).

Clause n. 3 explains that a predicate or n-ary predicate constant P of L denotes an operator **p** that, following the perception of certain circumstances, delivers as output the set of the objects to which P applies in those specific circumstances, i.e. in that situation and at that time. If P = "eats", the corresponding MoR **p** is the operator that, given a particular circumstance, singles out the objects that eat in said circumstance, that is, relatively to that situation and to that time. [68]

---

[68] In the definition we have just examined, proper nouns (corrisponding to the individual constants of L) are treated as non-rigid designators. However, according to a very well-known, and generally accepted thesis formulated by the greatest logician alive (Saul Kripke), names operate in the natural language as *rigid designators*. A rigid designator is an expression that designates the same object in all circumstances (times + situations) and, in particular, in counterfactual circumstances (when I say "Jacopo Tagliabue could have become a painter" it is always Jacopo Tagliabue I am talking *of*, even though the circumstance I am taking into account is different from @).

It is technically very easy to capture within our formalization such aspect of the functioning of

A1.2.2.1 Meaning of individual terms

We are now able to provide a recursive characterization v_a of the meaning of all the singular terms of the language. v_a is the combination of the interpretation operator v, and the assignment operator a, assigning values to the variables of L, which is defined via recursion as follows:

(B)
1.   If v is an individual variable of L, then $v_a(v) = a(v)$;
2.   If c is an individual constant of L, then $v_a(c) = v(c)$.

(P)
1.   If f is an n-ary constant funtor of L, and $t_1, \ldots t_n$ are terms, then
     $v_a(f(t_1, \ldots t_n)) = v(f)(v_a(t_1), \ldots , v_a(t_n))$.

A1.2.2.2 Meaning of formulas, truth, validity, logical consequence

Once the terms of L have been assigned a meaning, we can as well assign a meaning to the formulas of L. The function v here will assign as meaning, to every formula α of L, an operator from pairs of circumstances (which are, in turn, pairs <situation, time>) and assignments to $\{1, 0\}$. In other words, the definition of the meaning of a formula has the following general form:

(D) If α is a formula of L , then $v(\alpha) = e\colon \mathbf{C} \times \mathbf{A} \to \{1, 0\}$

where $\mathbf{A} = \{a_1, \ldots, a_n\}$ the set of the assignments of values to the variables, and $\mathbf{C}$ is still $\mathbf{W} \times \mathbf{T}$.

---

ordinary language: it will suffice to stipulate that all the MoR c constituting the meaning of nouns or individual constants are constant-output operators, i.e. in any circumstance they always indicate the same object as output or bearer of the name. The same holds for constant functors as well.

If we accept that names and functors are rigid designators, then the first two clauses can be simplified: it would be enough to impose the interpretation operator v directly assigns objects and, respectively, operators, to those types of symbols, without going through c and k. In this case, the clauses can be riformulated as follows:

1a.   If c is a noun or individual constant of L, then $v(c) = d \in \mathbf{D}$.

2a.   If f is a functor or n-ary constant functor of L, then $v(f) = f\colon \mathbf{D}^n \to \mathbf{D}$.

The meaning of a formula of L is an operator, i.e. a MoR, **e**, that, given a certain circumstance and assigment of values to the variables, produces as output 1 if and only if that formula "says how things stand" (in that particular circumstance, and in relation to that assignment). According to our perspective,"truth" cannot but mean "adequate description of the real", and this is precisely what is done by a proposition that says how thing stand. Therefore, 1 can be seen as a placeholder for true and 0 as a placeholder for false (hence, our formal semantics is bivalent, but modifying it, if necessary, would not be complicated, for example, to represent phenomena of the ordinary language such as vagueness).

As Wittgenstein states in proposition 4.024 of the Tractatus logico-Philosophicus: "To understand a proposition means to know what is the case, if it is true". Informally, this signifies that to grasp the meaning of a formula of L means to know in which circumstances it results true, and in which it does not, namely (from our point of view) to be endowed with a MoR that operates by appropriately associating that formula to the circumstances in which it results true.

Thus, the extended definition of the meaning of the formulas of L presented below consists in a series of recursive clauses that are completely analogous to those established in a Tarski-style semantics, and that characterize the behaviour of **v**. The recursion base (B) assigns a meaning to each atomic formula; then, in the recursive step (R), the meaning of the compound formulas is defined on the basis of the meaning of their constituents.

For the sake of notational simplicity, we will directly relativize **v** to situations, to times and to assignments. Namely, we will write expressions of the form: "$v(\alpha)$**w, t, a** $= s$", to indicate that the meaning of α is the MoR that, "perceiving" the situation **w**, the time **t** (hence, the circumstance **c** $= $ <**w, t**>) and the assignment **a**, gives as output $s \in \{1, 0\}$, i.e. $s = 1$ or $s = 0$.

Furthermore, we will denote by "**a**[x/**d**]" the x-variant **d** of assignment **a**. The x-variant **d** of **a** is simply the assignment of values to the variables which is identical to **a**, except for the fact that it assigns to the variable x the individual **d** $\in$ **D**.

Finally, here is the recursive definition (obviously, it all should be relativized also to the model M, but we can take it as implicit, thus not include it in the notation):

(B)

1. $v(P(t_1, \ldots, t_n))$**w, t, a** $= 1$ if and only if $< v_a(t_1), \ldots, v_a(t_n)> \in v(P,$ **w, t**$)$

(P)

1. $(\neg\alpha)$**w, t, a** $= 1$ if and only if $v(\alpha)$**w, t, a** $= 0$

2. $v(\alpha \wedge \beta)$**w, t, a** $= 1$ if and only if $v(\alpha)$**w, t, a** $= 1$ and $v(\beta)$**w, t, a** $= 1$

3. $v(\alpha \vee \beta)$**w, t, a** $= 1$ if and only if $v(\alpha)$**w, t, a** $= 1$ or $v(\beta)$**w, t, a** $= 1$

4. $v(\alpha \rightarrow \beta)$**w, t, a** $= 1$ if and only if $v(\alpha)$**w, t, a** $= 0$ or $v(\beta)$**w, t, a** $= 1$

5. $v(\alpha \leftrightarrow \beta)$**w, t, a** $= 1$ if and only if $v(\alpha)$**w, t, a** $= v(\beta)$**M, w, t, a**

6. $v(\Box\alpha)$**w, t, a** $= 1$ if and only if for each $<w_1, t_1> \in$ **C**, $v(\alpha)$**w, t, a** $= 1$

7. $v(\Diamond\alpha)$**w, t, a** $= 1$ if and only if for some $<w_1, t_1> \in$ **C**, $v(\alpha)$**w, t, a** $= 1$

8. $v(F\alpha)$**w, t, a** $= 1$ if and only if for some $t_1 \in$ **T** $: t < t_1$, $v(\alpha)$**w, t_1, a** $= 1$

9. $v(P\alpha)$**w, t, a** $= 1$ if and only if for some $t_1 \in$ **T** $: t_1 < t$, $v(\alpha)$**w, t_1, a** $= 1$

10. $v(\forall x\alpha)$**w, t, a** $= 1$ if and only if for each **d** $\in$ **D**, $v(\alpha)$**w, t, a**$[x/d]$ $= 1$

11. $v(\exists x\alpha)$**w, t, a** $= 1$ if and only if for each **d** $\in$ **D**, $v(\alpha)$**w, t, a**$[x/d]$ $= 1$

12. $v([\lambda x.\alpha])$**w, t, a** $= \{$**d** $\in$ **D** $\mid v(\alpha)$**w, t, a**$[x/d] = 1\}$

13. $v([\lambda x.\alpha](t))$**w, t, a** $= 1$ if and only if $v(\alpha)$**w, t, a**$[x/d] = 1$, with **a**$[x/d](x) = v_a(t)$

Starting from this definition, we can then provide the standard Tarskian truth-definition for a formula α in a model M, and, through this, the notions of *logical validity* and *logical consequence* as well:

- A formula α of L is *true* in a model M, in respect to a situation **w** and a time **t**, iff, for every assignment **a**, $v(\alpha)$**w, t**, a $= 1$. We write:

M, w, t $\models \alpha$

- A formula α of L is *logically valid* iff it is true in every model M, situation **w**, and time **t**. We write:

$\models \alpha$

- Given a set **F** of formulas of L, $\mathbf{F} = \{\alpha_1, \ldots, \alpha_n\}$, and a formula β of L, β is a logical consequence of **F** iff in every model M, situation **w**, time **t** and assignment **a**, if for every $\alpha \in F$, $v(\alpha)$w, t, a $= 1$, then $\mathbf{v(\alpha)}$**w, t, a** $= 1$. We write:

$\mathbf{F} \models \alpha,$

Or for brevity:

$\alpha_1, \ldots, \alpha_n \models \alpha.$

Many other linguistic relations, such as that of presupposition, that of equivalence, etc., can be characterized in terms of the mathematical formalism just introduced.

A1.2.3 Specifications on the semantics

Let us introduce some clarifications concerning the functioning of the assigment operator **a** that assigns values to variables. According to the semantics, the individual variables of L fulfill the same thematic role that in the ordinary language is occupied by pronouns, namely, the referential expressions (suppose, of English) used to refer to individuals, such as "he", "they", etc. The operator **a**, which ascribes determinate values to the variables by assigning objects to them, corresponds to something like those acts of pointing, by means of which, in the ordinary language, the value of non-anaphoric pronouns (i.e., not referring to an antecedent) is identified in given contexts.

It is in consideration of this that, within the model M, we have distinguished the operator **a** from the operator **v** that assigns meanings to the expressions of the language which are constants. Such a distinction effectively captures that trait of ordinary language causing constant expressions to maintain a definite meaning in a specific context (on account of certain conventions that are shared among the speakers in a given time, etc., "Jacopo Tagliabue" refers to Jacopo Tagliabue and not to someone else), whereas pronominal expressions ("him", "she", "he") can be used to refer to different individuals even within the same context. Hence, "it can be helpful to think of [**a**] as fixing the value of each variable much as an act of ostension can fix the value of an antecedent-less third-person pronoun". [69]

Moreover, we notice that to *specific types of linguistic expressions are effectively associated, as their meanings, specific types of MoR*. For instance, the standard logical connectives are (symbols having as meaning) operators from truth-values to truth-values; and the standard quantifiers, corresponding to the English expressions "all", "some", "a few", "none", are in turn operators, that is, MoR. These can be conceived as instructions that algorithmically evaluate the assignments of values to the variables they bind: a quantifier indicates how many assignments of value must give the value 1. Therefore, in this context, a quantifier designates, so to speak, kind of a second-order MoR. If, according to our recursive definition, "$P(x)$" denotes the first-order operator or MoR that, given in input certain circumstances of the model, yields as output 1 if and only if the object, which (in that assignment) is the value of x, is one of the things that are P (in those circumstances, etc.); then, in "$\exists x P(x)$", "$\exists x$" indicates a second-order MoR, i.e. one operating on the first-order MoR $P(x)$: and such second-order MoR gives in output 1 if and only if the first-order MoR $P(x)$ gives in output 1 for at least one assignment of value to x.

A1.2.4 Computability of the semantics

Perhaps the most remarkable result, with respect to the mathematics of the MoR, is that a thoroughly recursive semantics for our language is rendered possible by this mathematical structure. Once the basic expressions of the language have been assigned meanings within a certain

[69] Chierchia and McConnell-Ginet [1990], p. 125.

model, the meaning of compound expressions can be recursively computed starting from those. Formuals of indefinite complexity can always be recursively evaluated in a finite number of steps.

Futhermore, note that the parallelism between syntax and semantics is rigorously respected: the recursive clauses of the semantics presented above perfectly correspond to the recursive clauses of the syntax of L exposed in Chapter 2 (and since the semantics of the formulas mirrors their syntactic form, and the syntax is wholly computable, one expects also the semantics to be).

A1.3 Primitive MoR, derived MoR

We conclude this appendix with some glosses on the semantic interdefinability of various MoR. On the grounds of the recursive structure presented, the formal language L results to be, from a semantic standpoint, partially "redundant" (however, in a way that is congruent with the standards of the current logical-mathematical formalisms). In fact, some of the symbols of L are definable through, and therefore, reducible to, others on the basis of the operators they express. For instance, the symbol "→", which denotes a logical operator (and hence, MoR), corresponds to what in the literature is referred to as "material conditional". Its behaviour is completely captured by a combination of **conjunction** and **negation**, and we know that AND and NOT can be implemented in our intended model by every single cell thanks to the super-rule ϕ capable of universal computation, as analyzed in Chapter 1. This can be illustrated by means of the familiar truth tables derived by the recursive clauses of the semantics we have just examined:

α	β	$\alpha \to \beta$			$\neg$	$(\alpha$	$\wedge$	$\neg$	$\beta)$
1	1	1	1	1	1	1	0	0	1
1	0	1	0	0	0	1	1	1	0
0	1	0	1	1	1	0	0	0	1
0	0	0	1	0	1	0	0	1	0

This implies that we are able to define the material conditional operator as follows:

$$\alpha \to \beta =_{df} \neg(\alpha \wedge \neg\beta);$$

Stated in terms of MoR, this means that we could define the MoR *material conditional* through the MoR (boolean) *conjunction* and (boolean) *negation*. Fundamentally, a MoR is what it does, and what *material conditional* does can be precisely replicated by what is done by an adequate combination of (boolean) *conjunction* and (boolean) *negation*. As is well-known, the standard Boolean operators are characterized by many other simple interdefinability results (for example, each of these forms a functionally complete set: $\{\neg, \wedge\}$, $\{\neg, \to\}$, $\{\neg, \vee\}$, etc.); or rather, they can all be simulated by a single operator (the Sheffer bar). In line with our conventionalist perspective, any choice is acceptable, provided that clarity is maintained in the definitions and stipulations that follow from said choices. The selection of the operators responds to criteria of convenience and notational efficiency.

The same holds for the two operators corresponding to □ and ◊; on the basis of the recursive clauses of the semantics, each can be defined (and here, only a generic knowledge of modal logic is required) in terms of the other as follows:

$$\square =_{df} \neg\Diamond\neg;$$

$$\Diamond =_{df} \neg\square\neg;$$

Namely, in terms of MoR, *necessary* means *not-possible-*(that)*not*, and **possible** signifies *not-necessary-*(that)*not*. The availability of both is merely a matter of convenience: in consideration of the parallelism between syntax and semantics characterizing our formal framework, the fact that each of the two MoR is definable by means of a combination of the other and the MoR (boolean) *negation*, implies the substitutability of the symbol "◊" of our formal language L with the string of symbols F ¬□¬", etc. in any context.

Vice versa, some operators have not been listed among the basic symbols of the language, but they may easily be inserted by defining them starting from those. If we wish to have a stronger conditional operator than *material conditional* available, for instance a strict conditional such as the one introduced by C.I. Lewis, it will suffice to introduce a symbol – let us assume, " ▶" – into the language by means of the following definition:

$$\alpha \blacktriangleright \beta =_{df} \Box(\alpha \rightarrow \beta).$$

This definition, through the recursive clauses of the semantics governing the behaviour of the operators $\Box$ and $\rightarrow$, tells us that ▶ corresponds to an operator, say **strict conditional**, which gives in output 1, if and only if the operator **material conditional** $\rightarrow$ yields in output 1 in every circumstance of the model, i.e. in every situation or configuration of the universe, and in every time.

Alternatively, by means of the operators F and P, we can define other temporal operators such as the following:

$$S_P =_{df} \neg P\neg;$$

$$S_F =_{df} \neg F\neg;$$

"S_P" denotes the MoR **always in the past**, or **it has always occurred that**, whereas "S_F" expresses the MoR **always in the future**, or **it will always occur that**, which involves a universal quantification (restricted to the past and to the future, respectively) over the discrete instants of time included within our structure.

A2 Graphene

This appendix represents a digression in a highly "theoretical" volume such as this one, for it adopts an application-oriented outline of some of the recent advancements in the field of nanotechnologies. One may ask what might be the connection between the physical-mathematical model presented in the previous chapters and nanotechnological research. The answer to this question is offered by *graphene* and, specifically, by the nice analogies between this material and the intended model of our mathematical theory of the MoR.

The name "graphene" comes from the contraction of "graphite + ene", and the term is used to indicate a two-dimensional layer of carbon atoms, which is one-atom thick. Graphene, like diamond, is pure carbon, and it has been systematically studied only since 2004. Graphite – that can also be found in an ordinary pencil – simply consists in a compound of graphene layers piled one on top of each other: the bonds between one layer and another are much weaker than those between the atoms of the same layer, and for this reason it is deemed that small flakes of graphene are produced by exfoliation even in the trace left by your favourite pencil. On the other hand, at present it is rather hard to artificially produce pure layers of graphene, and such difficulty causes graphene to be one of the most expensive materials in the world (though its cost is rapidly decreasing)!

Then, it might appear surprising that researchers are so concerned with something that is so thin and costly. The explanation to this fact rests on the unusual properties of this material: for example, with a resistance to breaking 200 times greater than that of steel, it is one of the most resistant materials currently known.

However, what we are interested in is the *informational* aspect of graphene. A graphene sheet (devoid of impurities) precisely consists of a two-dimensional lattice of carbon atoms hexagonally arranged. Possible pentagons and hectogons count as impurities, nonetheless, they can theoretically (as we write, the processing of this material is still in an initial phase) be introduced to create natural deviations from the planarity of the sheet, thereby forming cones, curves, etc. Obviously, the hexagonal structure would constitute, in itself, a fairly extrinsic and fortuitous analogy to our hexagonal cells. Nevertheless, the case is that graphene is a semiconductor, and on top of that, a semiconductor with zero gap. Each carbon atom in a sheet of this material has one orbital *s* and three orbitals *p*. The orbital *s* and two of the three *p*s form the strong covalent bonds that render the hegagonal structure so resistant, while the third *p* constitutes the conduction band.

Now, also at ordinary temperatures, in the order of 20° centigrades, graphene displays outstanding electron mobility: it conducts electricity at a velocity 100 times higher than the silicon of computer chips, with very low levels of thermal dispersion and "noise". These features make it an ideal candidate for the construction of logical circuits and processors, and it is already conjectured that in the medium run it will dethrone silicon as the predominant semiconductor (possibly through the intermediate solution of "mixed" processors with silicon base and graphene multipliers). At the end of 2008, IBM announced that it had realized transistors based on our material with an operational speed in the order of gigahertz. Furthermore, researches on the possibility of constructing virtually eternal memories made of graphene have begun to take off.

At this point, it is legitimate to ask where these prodigious properties come from. And here comes the interesting part: the electronic structure of graphene is such that, in six points of each of its hexagonal cells, small quantities of energy are *linearly* dispersed (in more precise terms: the energies of the valence band and conduction band are linear functions of the momentum). The electrons on the hexagonal edges behave *as if they had no mass*. They move at a constant and very high velocity (in the order of 10^6 m/s!), as Dirac particles devoid of mass: specifically, as the relativistic fermions described by the Dirac equation for particles with spin ½.

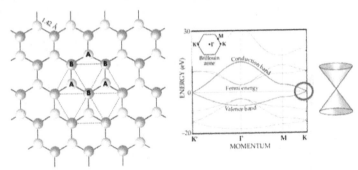

In other words: differently from conventional materials in which the velocity of electrons is related to their energy, in graphene the free electrons move linearly along the hexagonal cells, behaving as if they were photons whose velocity does not depend on the energy – with a uniform motion that is precisely analogous to that of the bits of our cells!

Now, it is not improbable to conjecture that there subsists a direct and precise connection between the velocity at which the electrons move linearly in graphene, their behaviour as mass-less, and the extremely low energy dispersion: as it is known from the very first Chapter of the book, from a physical-informational standpoint, we can find respectable conjectures to the effect that higher computational efficiency is one and the same with lower energetic and "entropic" dissipation associated with the movement of information bits. That is why we devised the super-rule φ underlying our cellular automaton, as it guarantees universal computation and strong reversibility, and thus, total preservation of information.

Obviously, the hexagonal atomic structure of graphene, however microscopic, is located at much higher dimensional levels than those at which we have conjecturally placed our elementary cells that are bit conductors. Hence, of course, a graphene sheet is not at all a layer of "the ultimate atoms of the universe": its cells are "too big", its electrons, however fast, are still way far from the speed of light, etc.

On the other hand, if the physical-mathematical structure that is investigated in this work actually possesses a fractal nature, i.e. it is found to be isomorphic in different dimensional orders, then the isomorphism between our theoretical cells and those of graphene – as far as its behaviour is presently known – is truly remarkable. While hexagonal cellular automata are not very popular in the literature, in view of the potential offered by graphene's unique properties, research in physics on this type of computational structure is already going on. On *Applied Physics Letter*, Chilean researchers have recently published the results of a real implementation of a cellular automaton with cells composed of graphene nanoribbons.[70] In particular, the scientists showed the feasibility of transmitting binary information in such a cellular automaton: in fact, the propagation must not occur at special temperatures, graphene does not need to be "cut" into unconventional shapes and the method is fully scalable (i.e. it does not lose computationally salient properties as the size of the graphene nanoribbons varies). The definition of universal logical gates, on these same structures, is by now an established fact.

It is now difficult to predict the future convergence (if there will be one) between the advancements in the physics of nanomaterials (and their industrial application) and the theoretical research on the computational properties of regular hexagonal lattices. Certainly, although the conspicuous affinities between these two research paths do not prove that such fields are *de facto* closely connected, we are however able, for the first time and on sound scientific basis, to stipulate the possibility that they are indeed so, with significant theoretical and applicative implications on both sides.

---

[70] See León, Barticevic and Pacheco [2009].

A3 Biology

A3.1 Computation in the cells: *wetware*

Cellular biology, *prima facie*, studies a fluid, continuous world in evolution and in physical motion. An amoeba that splits, a DNA filament that unwinds, a white cell that attacks a bacterium: all these phenomena appear as analogic, continous events analogous to any other process that can be found in nature also at higher levels of complexity. If these processes were to be mathematically represented, it seems that we would have to employ continous value functions, and not discrete sequences.

However, this appearance should not be emphasized. We know that, conforming to our underlying mathematical option, the essence of the world is discrete and the continuum is just appearance emerging at higher level. On the other hand, modern biology is based on the fundamental idea that what animals and plants are composed of is *discrete* units: the cells. For example, DNA, with respect to the functions fundamental to life it performs, is a completely discrete structure as it contains four nucleotides, A, C, T, and G, in discrete and well-defined sequences (they could be codified in two bits: A as 00, C as 01, T as 10, and G as 11, and a double helix of DNA would result in a double sequence of bits that could be scrolled within our hexagonal- cell computational model...). Now, in his recent book *Wetware*, the biologist Dennis Bray has defined as wetware the set of the computational processes occurring in the living cells,[71] and has proposed the philosophical conjecture that life itself, and in particular, the activity of any cell – whether unicellular organisms or components of multicellular organisms of any complexity, from a larva to a sequoia to a mammal – *consists* in this set of computations. This thesis forms the core of the (relatively) new branch of molecular biology which is called *systems biology*.

It is simple to recognize the complete coherence between this approach

---

[71] It must be borne in mind that, in the literature, the term "wetware" is also used to indicate the interaction between human brain and cerebral software.

and the one underpinning our research on the mathematics of the MoR. First of all, life in the cells consists in their being *systems* that implement *models of reference*: if the hypothesis of wetware is correct, it can be justifiably held that the living cells encode an *internal representation* of the surrounding world of which they *perceive* what is immediately close to them, i.e. the *neighbourhood* (and note that *system, internal/external,* etc., are notions defined in axiomatic form in Chapter 3 of this book, and that *perception* and *neighbourhood* are two cardinal notions of our theory of the MoR, as it has been implemented in our discrete universe from Chapter 1).

Furthermore, the cells compute these perceptions through circuits that perform logical operations, and they produce *actions* as output. In the words of Bray:

> For all their small size and (apparent) simplicity, single-celled organisms are neverthless complete functional systems. I would argue that any animal large or small that pursues a freely moving existence must have some minimal level of internl organization in order to survive. It has to detect and recognize salient features of its environment, move to a suitable niche, detect and hunt down prey, sense and avoid predators, find a mate. A flood of information enters such a cell every second of its existence through its membrane. This must be assimilated, sorted, codified. The cell has to choose one integrated, coherent action that ensures survival [...]. Certainly the general notion of computability will help as we unpack the molecular basis of why cells act as they do.[72]

Particular attention must be paid to the meaning of these statements: it is not only maintained that, in systems biology, the behaviour of the cells can be simulated by means of computational models, such as our cellular automaton, for example. Rather, what is argued is that the biological reality of the cells *consists* in their being information processors. For researchers it is totally reasonable to employ mathematical models to study and predict biological phenomena. The bottom-line thesis is that the living cells are *systems* (in the sense of **system** we formulated in this book: aggregates that are topologically connected according to the axioms of the ontology of the MoR) that implement MoR; namely, that also at this level of reality there exists an isomorphism betweem the physical world (specifically, biological) and the informational world.

---

[72] Bray [2009], pp. 25-6.

Let us start by examining some concrete examples of how simple unicellular organisms implement MoR, that is, deterministic sequences <perception, thought, action>.

A3.2 MoR in the unicellular organisms

At the most elementary level of life, we find the prokaryotic bacteria – basic units devoid of a true nucleus. Bacteria are only endowed with a few proteins and DNA agitated by the molecular motion in the cytosol. Nonetheless, a bacterium such as *escherichia coli* implements MoR enabling it to *perceive* several chemical substances as inputs, and *act* in two different ways. Some substances, such as sugars and amino acids perceived in input, cause the action that could be termed *attraction*: flagella (i.e. the small lashes on the surface of the bacterial cell) propel a local motion in the direction corresponding to the superficial side from which the substances are perceived. On the contrary, the perception of acids and other "unwelcome" chemical substances produce the action of repulsion: flagella act as to maximize the distance between the bacterium and the dangerous source.

As a consequence, *escherichia coli* also has a short-term *internal memory*: at time $t+1$ (obviously, on a higher temporal scale with respect to that of the atomic instants composing the time of the universe at base level), it must store in memory precise values for the situation of the surrounding chemical environment, the *neighbourhood*, as it was at t. It must do so to compare the values of the input perceived at $t+1$ (say i), with those of the input perceived at t (say, j): it has to compute the difference distributed between the two inputs $j-i$, and produce as action the motion in the direction d where the difference is relevant, if it is positive ("increase in good substances from the side d"), or the escape from that direction, if the relevant difference is negative ("increase in bad substances from the side d").

In sum, *escherichia coli* implements a MoR that is a conditional routine. If a bacterium is capable of this, we can reasonably expect more articulated behaviour from eukaryotic, namely nucleus-endowed, cells. And indeed it is what we find in reality. For instance, a typical amoeba *proteus*, as it is a predator organism that feeds on other unicellular organisms, cannot make do with local motion towards chemical substances: its preys are in turn capable of organized motion. Moreover, the amoeba performs differentiated activities at different times: it won't go hunting a paramecium while it is dividing in half, and neither when it has just englobed one and it is feeding on it. This means that the amoeba *proteus* possesses an articulated series of internal states, such as "looking for a prey", "rest", "halving", etc., and that the same perceived input (for example, "paramecium presence") gives rise to different actions depending on the internal states of the amoeba: hence, we are not very far from any one Turing machine, in which the action is not determined solely by the input perceived, but also by the ordered pair <*perception, internal state* >.

The tiny *stentor* (i.e. a long-shaped protozoon living attached to plants or other surfaces), provides us with another example of the relevance of possessing a short-term memory when it perceives an irritating substance. It typically responds to the input "irritating substance" firstly by bending on one side to ease the perception; if this action fails to alleviate the intensity of the input, its MoR activate a different action: the stentor starts turning over two or three times in rapid succession. If neither this action modifies the input, the protozoon undertakes a third action by contracting into itself and shortening. This implies that, since different outputs are produced starting from the same input, the *stentor* retains memory of the fact that an action has been previously attempted, and such fact must be codified in its internal states. The repeated application of the same stimulus produces a response that varies over time.

To conclude, the case of the simplest unicellular organisms shows that the cells exhibit two characteristics captured by our mathematics of the MoR: firstly, (a) from the standpoint of our conventionalist ontology, they are *systems*: aggregates of parts that are interconnected in such a manner that the distinction **external/internal** formulated a few chapters ago applies to them with a certain stability over time; secondly, (b) from an informational viewpoint, the cells have some knowledge of the state of affairs in their surrounding environment (namely, perceptions, whose type depends on the relevant MoR— we elaborate on this issue below), and and they process – think– this information thereby producing actions. They also possess internal states , and a memory, and these combined determine the appropriate actions.

A3.3 Cellular perception

Perception is thus a fundamental aspect of life and, as it results from the analysis conducted so far, it can be encountered from its most elementary forms: from our dear *escherichia coli*, prokaryote organisms are capable of perceiving their surrounding environment. Of course, this does not mean that unicellular organisms are endowed with capabilities as those we would term high-level "consciousness", or "comprehension". However, what results clear is that they are, in a precise sense, aware of the surrounding environment: they perceive this environment, in the specific sense of "perception" we have defined, and quantitatively characterized, in this work: a modification in the internal states of a system (in this case, a cell) over time which is caused by a modification in external states.

Another significant aspect of the knowledge of the world that can be possessed by a unicellular organism is, evidently, the selection of the stimuli. As we know from the formal definitions of Chapter 1, a MoR is defined over a precise set of perceptions, which it maps onto a specific set of actions in a deterministic manner. If a system implements a series of MoR, then these MoR directly determine what it can perceive: all the remainder of the surrounding occurrences are, from the standpoint of the system, negligible. *Escherichia coli* can perceive a certain set of chemical substances – this is the set over which its MoR are defined – and produce actions of movement towards something, or away from something. Other processes that occur in its *neighbourhood* are simply ignored.

To generalize: the cells have receptors in the border areas between the internal of the system they consist of , and the external world, each receptor is specialized in recognizing a specific chemical substance – a protein, a peptide, for instance: these are the relevant perceptions. Within our *framework*: the possible perceptions for a cell are nothing but the sets over which the MoR implemented by the cell are defined.

From this it follows that the internal representation of the external world which is realized, for example, by the system *escherichia coli*, is *selective*. Indeed our cell has an internal model of external reality, but this, however, is exactly a *model* – and it is so in the precise mathematical meaning of the term: a model of a reality x (for instance: a mathematical model of a network of interconnected computers, describing them in terms of sets, or of graphs) captures only *some* of the aspects of x — specifically, those relevant to the representation; and, it effectively represents them by means of a certain isomorphism: the correspondence between the structural attributes of the model and the structural attributes of the reality x that is represented therein.

A3.4 Protein transistors

The logical circuits of the computational activity performed within the cells are, first of all, macromolecules such as proteins. As it is well known since some decades, proteins can assume different *states*: a finite number of discrete states that manifest themselves, for example, in their physical conformation (haemoglobin has a certain form when it is bound to oxygen, in arterial blood, and a different one when it is not, in venous blood).

For the reason that they can assume different states, proteins and enzymes act as transistors — effectively, as conditional routings for signals, which deliver a certain output given an input and an internal state. Let us imagine to be an enzyme E. We are programmed to recognize a particular, rare molecule in our surrounding environment. We denote this substance by A: this is exactly a perception over which the implemented MoR is defined. As an enzyme, our task consists in selecting molecules of A in the environment, and our proper action is to transform them into molecules A'. However, we do not operate unconditionally, but rather only under the condition that we also perceive another molecule, B, which catalyzes the chemical reaction. This molecule's role is that of "activating" the operator or MoR in question. In the description of Bray:

> You, the enzyme, can adopt two different shapes. In one of these (call it your "on" state) you convert A to A' as just described. In the other, "off", state you are inert — unable to function as an enzyme. And how are these two states controlled? Why, by the binding of a second molecule, call it B. If B is absent, you are off, inactive: the pipeline conversion to A' cannot proceed. But if you meet and bind a B molecule, you flip to the on state and the reaction can occur.[73]

---

[73] Bray [2009], p. 66.

Therefore, our MoR is a simple conditional that (in the notation of our book) instantiates the schema:

$$\alpha \wedge \beta \rightarrow \alpha_1.$$

It can be seen that such functioning is not too dissimilar from that of any one of our elementary cells implementing the logical gate. Undoubtedly, any enzymatic reaction involves a very vast series of procedures, and conceivably, many of these processes are not fully known. However, if our general conventionalist perspective, according to which computation is "in the eye of who beholds", is valid, then, what counts is that it is possible to extract the relevant computation from an ampler computation into which the former is immersed: as we know from the § 1.9 of this volume, a pertinent operator f can always be found immersed into an operator g with higher ariety with respect to input and/or output, if some of these inputs have a constant or periodic character, and part of these outputs can be discarded as *garbage bits*.

It is shown by other, more complex, enzymatic reactions that proteins also realize the *fan-out* of signals, logical negation, and any other elementary computational operation. [74] Furthermore, the fact that the output or action of a protein can be the input of a topologically contiguous protein – in the exact same manner as the output of an elementary cell in our model is exposed to its neighbours that perceive it as output – leads us to understand first, that it is easy to have logical circuits realized by proteins; and second, that also at this level of chemical-biological description, the notion of MoR enable us to capture an isomorphism between physical reality and informational reality: the physical linkages of a sequence of enzymes and the chemical reactions undertaken by this chain, constitute, at the very same time, a process of computation: specifically, logical operations with the product of an enzyme, i.e. the action determined by a computation within the protein, which becomes the perception of the successive enzyme. At molecular level, the chemical reactions are one and the same with the physical motions, which in turn can be characterized as changes of state.

---

[74] See again Bray, pp. 80-1.

A3.5 *Copy*, complexity, recursion: in quest of the MoR *life*

At this point we ask ourselves: what are the specific MoR of *life*? In other words, what does the especial MoR that is **life** consist in and how can it be defined? Philosophers of biology and biologists argue over what constitutes life, nonetheless all agree upon the fact that surely life involves specific *processes*, such as the capacity of processually self-building and self-repairing, and that of self-replicating, namely, of creating *self-copies*.

Hence, **life** must involve the MoR *copy*: copy of part of self, copy of the whole self. Already in the 60's, Watson and Crick, the founding fathers of molecular biology, conjectured that RNA might have been the first molecule capable of self-replicating (labour division between DNA, RNA and proteins being a subsequent by-product of evolution). As it is well-known, the key to replication lies in the pairing of nucleotide bases, which allows the relevant molecules to duplicate themselves by catalyzing the free nucleotide bases thereby producing a complementary copy of themselves. Thus, a molecule of RNA is composed of both a quantity of information implemented in the physical structure of the molecule itself, and a series of functions and activities determined by that *same structure*...

In this construction we may perhaps catch a glimpse of self-reference. Our laboratory is working on the hypothesis that the MoR *life* must be a MoR realizing that specific type of self-reference that we called recursive, and formally defined in Chapter 4. Let us see why.

If the cells are systems that implement MoR, then we can justifiably state that they are computers, although not in the "classical" sense intended by von Neumann: they are non-standard processors that massively compute in parallel. The studies developed in the discipline termed *artificial life* (AL) are aimed at capturing (what we call) the essential MoR of life primarily by means of an appropriate *reverse engineering* of what occurs in the living forms, starting from the most elementary ones. And it should be stressed that the principle animating AL is totally congruous with the underlying assumption of the mathematics of the models of reference, that is, the structural identity between physical reality and information. In the words of Langton:

Only when we are able to view life-as-we-know-it in the larger context of life-as-it-could-be will we really understand the nature of the beast. Artificial Life is a relatively new field employing a synthetic approach to the study of life-as-it-could-be. It views life as a property of the organization of the matter, rather than a property of the matter which is so organized.[75]

It must be noted that, as the activity of the cells is characterized in terms of the implementation of MoR, these count as *adaptive agents in complex systems*. As we know, conforming to the theory of complex systems, complexity must emerge at higher level starting from simple agents instantiating simple rules. The analysis of the cellular activity which is proposed by Bray's *Wetware*, and captured in terms of our MoR, designate the organic cells as the basic blocks of complex systems according to the characterization formulated by Maes — i.e. systems in which an adaptive autonomous agent enjoys the following properties:

- *Interaction with the environment*: the agent *perceives* the environment (often complex and dynamic) with which it interacts through its sensors, and *acts* accordingly.
- *Goal-oriented actions*: the agent operates as to achieve certain goals (of which he may not be "conscious" at all, in a strict sense), such as the maximization of certain internal states, or simply self-preservation.
- *Thought*: the agent is able to internally process the information and to select the corresponding actions.
- *Adaptive dynamics*: the agent is able to anticipate future states and possibilities because it is endowed with internal memory and an internal model of the surrounding environment.[76]

John von Neumann himself, the earlier architect of cellular automata, had thought of discrete systems of elementary cells precisely in order to account for the phenomenon of self-replication, namely the capability of producing identical self-copies, which is at the very core of life (i.e. of the MoR *life*). For von Neumann the starting point was the observation that it is extremely difficult to artificially replicate the fact that in nature, reproduction allows *complexity* to be *conserved*. In general, the machines assembling other machines are more complex than those being assem-

---

[75] See Langton [1989].
[76] See Maes [1994] and Maes [1990].

bled, at least on account of the fact that they must contain, in some form, the *"blueprint"*, the project or the code, of the machine they are to assemble.

On the contrary, in nature, not only reproduction does not reduce complexity, but, in addition, the *blueprint* of what is replicated, and which is essential to the copy itself, is generally simpler than the finite product. For instance: human brain is capable of storing data for approximately one billion of billions bits. But the *blueprint* of human brain must be entirely included in the genome. And the genome contains eight hundred million bytes, with large redundancies, thus, once these have been "compressed", we are left with approximately from thirty and one hundred million bytes, i.e. less than 10^9 bits; for the sake of understanding, it is less than what is required by the software of Microsoft Word!

Therefore, we are already able to identify a first feature that is to emerge from a MoR *life*, or by a series of MoR capable of realizing the relevant theoretical role: what implements this MoR, or this series of MoR, must possess the capability of producing self-copies with no loss of complexity. If, as we are taught by *Wetware*, the simplest living forms are (complex!) biochemical machines, and such machines (as we my add) are alive and active by reason of their instantiating certain MoR, then their operating must be algorithmic. Analogous considerations had already led von Neumann to conclude that the relevant algorithm must be implementable by a universal Turing machine; therefore Turing machines capable of self-replication must be possible.

What is most relevant in terms of the mathematics of the MoR, as anticipated, is that the MoR *life* will certainly have to be a self-referential MoR (and hence, a *metamodel*, in the meaning of metamodel characterized in § 4.5.1. of our book); furthermore, on the basis of the research conducted in our laboratory, we maintain that it must be a *recursively* self-referential MoR, precisely conforming to the formalization of recursive mathematics encountered in chap.4 of this volume. The rationale behind this is not difficult to discern, in light of the algorithmic characterization of the fact that a living system, starting from the originary RNA, produces copies of *itself*.

Consider any one system – say, a cellular automaton, C, which we assume capable of producing an identical copy of itself, C_1. This implies that: (a) the *blueprint* of C_1 must, in some form, be included in C (presumptively, as a code of the structure of C_1, which can be decoded and read by C); but also (b) C must insert a copy of that same *blueprint* into C_1 during its construction – otherwise it would not be a self-copy, and thus we would not have self-replication: this is precisely that specific case of copy, in which the blueprint of C, B_C, is the same *blueprint* of C_1: $B_C = B_{C1}$.

Now, let us suppose that C perceives in input the *blueprint* B_C. If the automaton constructs a copy of C, it seems that it is not actually self-replicating, since the aggregate $C + B_C$ produces C, not $C + B_C$. And the situation cannot be adjusted by adding to the input B_C a description of B_C itself: now we have a system $C + B_C + B_C$ producing $C + B_C$ – and we find ourselves in a vicious regress. The problem stems from the fact that the data constituting the blueprint, and which must be perceived by the system, are at the same time (a) "active" instructions, namely, which must be carried out by undertaking the corresponding actions, and (b) "passive" information that, itself being a part of the system that is self-replicating, must be reproduced and incorporated into the copy.

Note that such problem is wholly analogous to that of recursive self-reference, as it is realized, for example, in a logical-formal system sufficiently powerful to express (primitive) recursive operators, such as the systems DP and Q we encountered in § 4.4: as it had been properly realized by Gödel in the construction of his celebrated self-referential undecidable statement, none of the formulas of the system can be literally self-referential, in the sense of encompassing an exact copy of itself within it, for in order do so it should be bigger than itself. [77]

---

[77] Here is an informal example: any self-referential proposition, let it even be formulated in our ordinary language, can never explicitly and completely mention itself (supposedly, includindg all the linguistic signs that compose the proposition itself, in the same order and enclosed between quotation marks), because in order to to so it should be longer than itself. If we attempt to quote a proposition within itself in our ordinary language, we may obtain things such as:

(S) The proposition "The proposition is composed of seven words" is composed of seven words,

and it is evident that (S) does not refer to itself. (S) refers to the statement "The proposition is composed of seven words" and, stating that *this latter* is composed of seven words, (S) is true. In

The solution consists in the construction of a fixed point, whose admissibility is guaranteed by the validity, within the mathematics of the MoR, of the Fixed Point Theorem that was introduced in § 4.8. of our book: it is always possible to define self-referential recursive MoR that include their own code in their recursive definition. Specifically, we know that the MoR *life*, inasmuch as it encompasses the concept of *identical copy of itself*, will at least have to include a structure of this form in its definition.

Therefore, in the case of a self-replicating system, it will be required to have a structure such as the following, which reproduces the one originally furthered by von Neumann for his automaton:

- We take a system C^1, which copies any *blueprint* B it perceives in input;
- We define a system C^2, that inserts a copy of B into the system costructed by C;
- We term C^* the system resulting from the composition of C, C^1, and C^2, that is $C^* = C + C^1 + C^2$;
- Now obviously C^* will have its blueprint, say, B_{C^*};
- Let now C^δ be the system C^* with B_{C^*} perceived as input *by* C.

At this moment, it can be seen that C^* is effectively a system capable of self-reproduction. And no vicious circle is involved because C^* already exists *before the blueprint* B_{C^*} itself is defined.

Attention should be drawn to a significant point that only few notice: the isomorphism between the strategy adopted here by von Neumann and the Gödelian self-referential strategy. In a note to his famous paper on the incompleteness of arithmetics, Gödel described the self-referential character of his renowned self-referential undecidable statement in this terms:

Contrary to appearances, such a proposition involves no faulty circularity, for initially it only asserts that a certain well-defined formula (namely the one obtained [...] by a certain substitution) is unprovable. Only subsequently (and, so to speak, by chance) does it turn out that this formula is precisely the one

---

fact, "The proposition is composed of seven words" is effectively composed of seven words. Instead, (S) is not composed of seven words. Hence, (S) does not refer to the proposition (S), i.e. to itself: it says something true of a proposition different from itself.

by which the proposition itself was expressed.[78]

Parenthetically, while the original cellular automaton, capable of self-reproduction conceived by von Neumann required several thousands of elementary cells, and 29 states per cell, more recent automata, such as those elaborated by Langton and Byl, are self-replicating while being constituted by spaces with few tens of cells having only six states.[79] This simplification leads us to conclude that the structure of the MoR life may be not excessively complicated, and if the conjectures developed in our laboratory prove to be correct, it will have to be a recursively self-referential MoR.

A3.6 *Life,* biology and nanotechnology

Furthermore, this is the point where the notion of *life*, namely the MoR *life*, may make the biological aspect of the MoR and the (nano)technological one converge. Von Neumann's cellular automaton, of which we stressed the connection with the recursive structure captured by the mathematics of the MoR, is deemed to be a pillar of the modern nanotechnological science, ever since Eric Drexler described a von Neumann-style (quasi-)universal constructor[80] in his Ph.d dissertation, which later evolved into the popular book *Engines of Creation* that represents the cornerstone of nanotechnology. Drexler's original assembler used atoms and molecular fragments as basic materials for its constructions. Recent studies commissioned by NASA to the company General Dynamics confirmed that molecular nano-assemblers may indeed possess the structure of discrete state cellular automata, according to a model that does not deviate much from the one proposed in this work; and such automata would demonstrably be capable of self-reproducing. The self-replication capacity of a nanorobotic assembler, i.e. the possibility of such assembler producing identical copies of itself, is precisely where one of the potentially dangerous aspects of nanotechnologies resides, to the point that the same Drexler proposed to impose limits to the design and production of self-replicating nanorobots. On

---

[78] Gödel [1931], p. 55.

[79] See Byl [1989].

[80] See Drexler [1986].

the other hand, it would seem that the key to understand the secrets and dangers of nanotechnological life, indeed lies in dwelling on the meaning of the concept of *life* itself, conforming to the approach adopted in our theory of the MoR. In the words of Ray Kurzweil:

> The ultimate existence proof of the feasibility of a molecular assembler is life itself. Indeed, as we deepen our understanding of the information basis of life processes, we are discovering specific ideas that are applicable to the design requirements of a generalized molecular assembler.[81]

---

[81] Kurzweil [2005], p. 232.

References

Bellotti L., Moriconi E., Tesconi L. [2001], *Computabilità. Lambda-definibilità, ricorsività, indecidibilità*, Carocci, Roma.

Bennett C. [1973], "Logical Reversibility of Computation", *IBM Jour. Res. Dev. 6*, pp. 525-32.

Berkelamp E.R., Conway J.H., Guy R.K. [1982], *Winning Ways for Your Mathematical Plays*, Academic Press.

Boolos G.S., Burgess J.P e Jeffrey R.K. [2002], *Computability and Logic*, Cambridge UP, Cambridge.

Bray D. [2009], *Wetware. A Computer in Every Living Cell*, Yale UP, New Haven, Conn.

Byl J. [1989], "Self-Reproduction in Small Cellular Automata", *Physica 34D*, pp. 295-9.

Canonico A. e Rossi G. [2007], *Semi-immortalità. Il prolungamento indefinito della vita*, Lampi di stampa, Milano.

Casalegno P. [1997], *Filosofia del linguaggio. Un'introduzione*, Carocci, Roma.

Casari E. [1997], *Introduzione alla logica*, Utet, Torino.

Casati R. e Varzi A.C. [1999], *Parts and Places. The Structure of Spatial Representation*, MIT Press, Cambridge, Mass.

Chierchia G. e McConnell-Ginet S. [1990], *Meaning and Grammar*, MIT Press, Cambridge, Mass.

Chomsky N. [1956], "Three Models for the Description of Language", *IRE Trans. Info. Theo.*, IT2, pp. 113-129.

Chomsky N. [1957], *Syntactic Structures*, Mouton, The Hague.

Chomsky N. [1992], "Language and Interpretation. Philosophical Reflections and Empirical Inquiry", in J. Earman (ed.), *Inference, Explanation, and Other Frustrations*, University of California Press, Berkeley, pp. 99-128.

Davidson D. [1984], "Theories of Meaning and Learnable Languages", in *Inquries Into Truth and Interpretation*, Oxford UP, Oxford.

Dennett D. [1989], *The Intentional Stance*, MIT Press, Cambridge, Mass.

Drexler E. [1986], *Engines of Creation. The Coming Era of Nanotechnology*, Anchor Books, Random House, New York.

Einstein A., Podolski B. e Rosen N. [1935], "Can Quantum Mechanical Description of Physical Reality Be Considered Complete?", *Phys. Rev. 37*, p. 777.

Fodor J. [1975], *The Language of Thought*, Harvester Press, hassocks.

Fredkin E. [1993], "A New Cosmogony", in PhysComp92, Los Alamitos, CA: Computer Society Press, pp. 116-121.

Fredkin E. e Toffoli T. [1982], "Conservative Logic", *International Journal of Theoretical Physics 21*, pp. 219-54.

Gardner M. [1970], "Mathematical Games: The Fantastic Combinations of John Conway's New Solitaire Game *Life*", *Scientific American*, 223, pp. 120-3.

Gödel K. [1931], "Über formal unentscheidbare Sätze der *Principia Mathematica* und verwandter Systeme I", *Monatshefte für Mathematik und Physik*, 38, pp. 173-98, tr. it. "Sulle proposizioni formalmente indecidibili dei *Principia Mathematica* e di sistemi affini I", in Shanker [1988], pp. 21-62.

Goodman N. [1956], *The Structure of Appearance*, Harvard U.P., Cambridge, mass., 3a ed. Reidel, Dordrecht 1977.

Groisman B., Ladyman J., Presnell S., Short T., [2007], "The Connection Between Logical and Thermodynamic Irreversibility", Studies in the History and Philosophy of Modern Physics, 38, pp. 58-79.

Hofstadter D. [1979], *Gödel, Escher, Bach:an Eternal Golden Braid*, Basic Books, NY.

Hofstadter D. [2007], *I Am a Strange Loop*, Basic Books, NY.

Ilachinski A. [2001], *Cellular Automata. A Discrete Universe*, World Scientific, Singapore.

Ingerson T.E. e Buvel R.L. [1984], "Structure in Asynchronous Cellular Automata", *Physica 10D*, pp. 59-68.

Kari J. [1990], "Reversibility of 2D Cellular Automata is Undecidable", *Physica D45*, pp. 379-85.

Kripke S. [1980], *Naming and Necessity*, Blackwell, Oxford.

Kurzweil R.[2007], *The Singularity is Near*, Duckworth, London.

Langton C.G. [1989] (a c. di), *Artificial Life*, Addison & Wesley, New Mexico.

León R.L., Barticevic Z., Pacheco M. [2009], "Graphene Nanoribbon Array in a Cellular Automata Architecture for Propagation of Binary Information", Applied Physics Letters 94, 173111, 1-3.

Lewis D.K. [1972], "General Semantics", in D. Davidson e G. Harman (eds.), *Semantics for Natural Language*, Reidel, Dordrecht.

Lewis D.K. [1986], *On the Plurality of Worlds*, Blackwell, Oxford.

Maes P. [1990] (ed)., *Designing Autonomous Agents: theory and Practice from Biology to Engineering and Back*, MIT Press.

Maes P. [1994], "Modeling Adaptive Autonomous Agents", *Artificial Life*, 1, pp. 135-62.

Marconi D. [2001], *Filosofia e scienza cognitiva*, Laterza, Roma-Bari.

Margolus N. [1984], "Physics-Like Models of Computation", *Physica 10D*, pp. 81-95.

Margolus N. [1988], *Physics and Computation*, Ph.D. Thesis, Tech. Rep. MIT.

Maroney O.J.E. [2005], "The (Absence of a) Relationship Between Thermodynamic and Logical Irreversibility", Studies in the History and Philosophy of Modern Physics, 36, pp. 355-74.

Montague R. [1973];, "The Proper Treatment of Quantification in Ordinary English", in R. Montague, *Formal Philosophy* (ed. da R. Thomason), Yale U.P. New Haven, 1974.

Myhill J. [1963], "The Converse of Moore's Garden of Eden Theorem", *Proc. Am. Math. Soc. 14*, pp. 685-6.

Penrose R. [1967], "Twistor Algebra", *J. Math. Phys. 8*, p. 345.

Rosen K. [2007], *Discrete Mathematics and Its Applications*, McGraw-Hill, New York.

Shanker S.G. [1988] (a c. di), *Gödel's Theorem in Focus*, Croom Helm, London, tr. it. *Il teorema di Gödel. Una messa a fuoco*, Muzzio, Padova 1991.

Shannon C.E. [1948], "A Mathematical Theory of Communication", *Bell System Technical Journal*, 27, pp. 379-423.

Shenker O., [2000], "Logic and Entropy", Philosophy of Science Preprint Archive, http://philsci-archive.pitt.edu/archive/00000115/.

Simons P.M. [1987], *Parts. A Study in Ontology*, Clarendon, Oxford.

Sipper M. [2004], *Evolution of Parallel Cellular Machines. The Cellular Programming Approach*, Springer.

Toffoli T. [1977], "Computation and Construction Universality of Reversible Cellular Automata", *Jour. Comp. Sys. Sci. 15*, p. 213.

Toffoli T. e Margolus N. [1990], "Invertible Cellular Automata: a Review", *Physica D45*, pp. 229-52.

Varzi A.C. [2003], "Mereology", *The Stanford Encyclopedia of Philosophy*, CSLI, Stanford.

Varzi A.C. [2005], "Change, Temporal Parts, and the Argument from Vagueness", *Dialectica*, 59, pp. 485-498.

Wang H. [1974], *From Mathematics to Philosophy*, Routledge & Kegan Paul, London.

Wittgenstein L. [1921], *Tractatus logico-philosophicus*, Routledge & Kegan Paul, London 1922.

Wolfram S. [2002], *A New Kind of Science*, Wolfram media.

Zuse K. [1982], "The Computing Universe", *Int. Jour. Of Theo. Phy. 21*, pp; 589-600.

Lightning Source UK Ltd.
Milton Keynes UK
UKOW05f2212060617

302843UK00008B/785/P